A
CAPITAL
OFFENCE

*The Plight of the
Young Single Homeless in London*

by

Brendan O'Mahony

ROUTLEDGE
11 New Fetter Lane, London EC4P 4EE

BARNARDOS
Tanners Lane, Barkingside, Essex IG6 1QG
1988

Dr Barnardo's
Tanners Lane, Barkingside, Ilford, Essex IG6 1QG

© Dr Barnardo's 1988

First published in Great Britain 1988

British Library Cataloguing in Publication Data

O'Mahony, Brendan
    A capital offence; the plight of the young, single, homeless
    on the streets of London.
    1. London. Homeless single young persons. Social
    conditions.
    I. Title II. Dr Barnardo's
    362.7

ISBN 0-415-03138-9

Typeset, printed and bound at the Barnardo Print Training
Scheme, Hertford, Herts.

Contents

systems–Difficulties facing Black communities–The responses of society and government

Preface

London. The name evokes images of a people, a way of life, a city depicting glories past and present. It is the home of Parliament, of a democracy that has been taken across the globe. It is a city of millions of people, of diverse cultures, a refuge for many driven out of their own lands by intolerance and persecution. For the tourist, it is a city rich in history and tradition, a city with a myriad of shops, theatres and restaurants. For many, London is the West End, Piccadilly Circus, the crowds and the bright lights.

Yet there is another London. Ralph McTell's song asks us to open our eyes and look at sights we would rather not see. There are

scenes of misery and distress that are an offence to the dignity
and humanity of another group of visitors to the West End. To
these people coming into the capital city, London is not a place
of bright lights or wonderment. It is a harsh, lonely and unwel-
coming place.

'Youth', wrote Thomas Cottle, 'becomes both the mirror on
which is recorded the images of our lives past and present and
the field on which the residues of our triumphs and incompletions
lie weakly asleep.' (Time's Children. Impressions of Youth.) A nation
can be judged by its youth. There are many bright, creative and
generous young people in London who mirror much of the good
in our society. The other side of that mirror reflects the incompletions of a nation that is often found wanting in the way in which
it cares for and cherishes its young.

There are other young people in London who are also bright,
creative and generous. They have left home for a whole variety
of reasons, but, as with all of us when we leave for the first time,
their primary purpose has been to follow their natural instincts
for independence and personal development. These young people
do not have the opportunity to develop their talents because they
are denied access to accommodation.

This book arose out of a report carried out over a six-month
period in 1987, the International Year of Shelter for the Homeless.
The report was commissioned by the London Division of Dr Barnardo's and its purpose was to look at what was happening to
young people homeless and at risk in Central London, to outline
the provision available for them, and to identify the gaps in
services.

The report was compiled within certain guidelines. The six-
month timetable means that it is not a complete and exhaustive
analysis of all London provision. The emphasis is on Central
London, though for practical purposes it does go beyond that strict
geographical area. Primarily, it is a piece of action research that
aims to give as clear a picture as possible of the issues involved
in working with this particular group of young people.

The literature survey, while not pretending to be a complete
overview, is an attempt to place the problems in a wider context
and give a better understanding of the difficulties facing these
young people. The interviews were chosen to give as wide a
spectrum as possible from all those involved, including policy
makers, managers, face-to-face workers and the young people
themselves. It is a representative but not an exhaustive list.

The first four chapters of the book, Part 1, look at the process of leaving home, what young people face when they reach London, the reasons for this, and what is presently being done to help them. The next four chapters outline some of the effects that being homeless has on groups of young people who are likely to be particularly vulnerable. Chapters 9 and 10 complete Part 2 by attempting to place the issues of drugs and prostitution in a wider context as a counter to the notion that all homeless young people must be part of those scenes. Part 3 looks at the future and outlines the ways forward in working with and for the young homeless as suggested both in the literature and by those who took part in the interviews.

If Thomas Barnardo were to return to London today he would no doubt be impressed by the advances and technology of the eighties. However, he would also have a sense of *déjà vu*. Beneath the veneer of our civilisation there is a great deal that has not changed from the time he began his work for the young in the mid-nineteenth century. Young people are still homeless, still sleeping out on the streets, still at risk from those who exploit their loneliness and distress.

It is hoped that this book will go some way to help people understand the plight of our young in the nation's capital. More importantly it is hoped that it might enable all those who have the power to care for our young people to make constructive interventions to ease that plight. Finally, this book is a testimony to all those agencies in London who, with often limited physical facilities and even fewer financial resources, have offered and continue to offer valuable services to some of the most needy and neglected young people in our society.

Brendan O'Mahony
March 1988

Acknowledgements

This book belongs to those individuals and agencies listed in the Appendices who welcomed me into their places of work and gave so generously of their time in a busy working day. Thanks are due especially to those young people in the agencies for their patience and forthrightness.

Some individuals are deserving of particular mention. To Emlyn Jones, Director, and the staff of the National Association of Voluntary Hostels for the time and assistance offered and in particular for the use of their office facilities in Covent Garden. To Sonia McIntosh of Ujima, Ossie Noblemunn of Mixifren and Brother Sam Symister of Harambee II for their generous input and assistance with some of the text. To Nic Fenton of the Mental Health Foundation for particular advice and assistance. To Mick Baker, Leader of the Soho Project, who gave a great deal of his time and practical help in gathering material. To Tom Murphy of *The Independent* newspaper for his assistance in gathering some of the literature. To Rob Murison of John Charcol Ltd for the welcome loan of the computer and word processing facilities. To the Turning Point organisation for permission to quote from *Going West* by Mark Lee *et al*. To Ritchie McMullan for permission to quote from *The Cycle of Sexual Abuse and Rape of Boys Involved in Prostitution*. To Routledge and Kegan Paul for permission to reproduce extracts from Brandon *et al*, *The Survivors*. To Weidenfeld and Nicolson for permission to reproduce extracts from Susanna Agnelli, *Street Children. A Growing Urban Tragedy*. To André Deutsch for permission to reproduce extracts from Gitta Sereny, *The Invisible Children: Child Prostitution in America, Germany and Britain*.

Particular thanks are due to my colleagues in Dr Barnardo's, London Division, who were the inspiration behind the original report and without whose continual encouragement and practical assistance none of this would have happened. Likewise I am particularly grateful to colleagues in the Library, in Research and Development, and in the Publicity department at Barnardo's Headquarters, as well as Jimmy James and all those at the Barnardo Print Training Scheme for their hard work in producing the book. Glen Plaster's work in preparing the photographs for the book is also much appreciated.

Finally, I am in debt to two ladies who made this book possible. To Helen Beltran, editor, for her expertise in putting all the material together and to the secretarial skills of Julie Cotton who typed the manuscript and all the scripts pertaining to the original report.

Brendan O'Mahony
March 1988

Part one

1 The process of leaving home

'British society is inconsistent in its attitudes towards young people. On the one hand, they are encouraged to show initiative, to seek opportunities away from home and set off in search of work. On the other, they are criticised if they move and find themselves homeless being considered useless, work-shy and abusers of the Social Security system.' (Barbara Saunders, *Homeless Young People in Britain. The Contribution of the Voluntary Sector.*)

Leaving home

Leaving home and making our own way in life is a process that is common to us all; that balancing of dependence and independence, until suddenly we feel ourselves to be far enough away and we are gone. For many of us, home supports that process and does not budge under the impact of our energies as we take our first steps and then finally move away. Many families have successfully coped with this developmental period in the lives of their young people, yet even in the best of them the balance between remaining together as a family and supporting this transition can be hard to maintain, without the pain and turmoil of leaving spilling over into division and premature separation.

Many young people leave home because they wish to do so and it is right both for them and for those with whom they live. As a group, however, they have no generalised rights to leave home – a fact substantiated by housing and incomes policies that take little heed of the natural desire of young people to break away and test out their skills in independent living.

Society accepts clearly enough the wish to move away to take up a job, to go to college or university or to join one of the services. The simple act of leaving home is difficult to acknowledge in its own right, however, and because of this the young who leave and become homeless are often castigated for doing so. They become victims of that stereotyping and discrimination which is born of ignorance and ambivalence and which is increasingly forcing many young homeless on to the margins of society.

The media image

Some of this ignorance has to do with the way in which the young are portrayed. Newspapers, especially, latch on to a particular stereotype that is both visible and easy to define. The spell of severe weather in January 1987 produced a crop of stories that highlighted the plight of such as *Carole,* a sixteen-year-old from Matlock, Derbyshire, who lived in a squat in Dalston, and *Alaistair,* twenty, who was begging and who also lived in a squat near the Oval. *William,* who begged on the Hungerford Bridge and lived in a cardboard box under the Queen Elizabeth Hall fitted this image, as did *Andrea,* the ex-drug addict and *Mary,* the fifteen-year-old Irish girl, slightly inebriated, sleeping on the pavements at Charing Cross.

Then there were the more frightening pictures that guarantee to keep the young homeless an unpopular cause and a low priority in society. *Boots* was described as a 'frightening unhinged skinhead girl, with a cross tattooed on her forehead, clad in tight denims, black jumper and fourteen-hole Doc Martins'. *Sean* was a 'jumpy-limbed, ginger-haired skinhead with the word "skins" needlessly tattooed on his forehead' and who 'exhaled an air of animal violence with every breath'. And there was *Sam* who 'wore an ankle-length, fake, silver-fox fur coat' and worked in 'a seedy hostess bar in Soho'.

These stories made good copy and, in truth, are not necessarily untypical of a particular section of young people who are homeless and at risk. It is a pity, however, that there is little mileage in the press for the stories of ordinary young people—stories that are not perhaps as vivid, but just as heart-breaking.

Views of homelessness

Misconceptions are not easy to counter.

There is a view often expressed that it is the fault of the young people if they find themselves without anywhere to live. This argument stresses that the young do not have to leave home, or, if they do, they do not have to go to areas where housing is at a premium. Nicholas Ridley, the Environment Secretary, expressed this view in Parliament in March 1987 when he urged the young homeless sleeping rough in London to move to areas of the country where homes were available. He backed up his argument with statistics, arguing that there were 760,000 more homes in Britain than there were households.

Those who see the reasons for homelessness as primarily politi-cal, social and economic, on the other hand, feel that it is just such a response that has caused such despair, misery and lack of provision. They believe that it is government policies that cause homelessness and only government has the power to respond substantially to the crisis. The young, it is argued, are political pawns, disenfranchised and forgotten because they have no voice to challenge a system that keeps them intentionally poor, homeless and with no chance of employment.

For others, homelessness and its accompanying difficulties are a direct result of the spiritual poverty in society, a poverty that cannot be alleviated by material provision alone. The young are poor in spirit and that kind of poverty is much more difficult to deal with effectively.

A further group would argue this point from a somewhat different perspective. They would equate homelessness not so much with spiritual poverty as with pathology and point to the inadequacies of the long-term homeless in society. So many are seen to be socially inadequate, psychologically disturbed and incapable of coping.

There is some validity in each of these views, though they do not in themselves fully explain the difficulties facing so many young people. Leaving home is a complex process and many factors come into play, not least the desire to escape from home and assert independence.

The process of leaving
Common to all homeless people has been the decision to move away from home. Leaving home is a complex process no matter what stage of life one is at. It may often have as much to do with the stage the individual has reached in his or her development as a young adult, as with prevailing personal, social and economic factors.

Often the young leave home as a result of a snap decision taken in response to some crisis. Little time is given for second thoughts or for questioning what ought to be done next. By nature the young act rather than reflect, and the young homeless are characterised by a desire to live for the moment, content to survive the day, with often little or no thought for the next.

What is clear, however, both from discussions with the young homeless themselves and with the agencies working with them, is that the decision to leave is often viewed not as an act of despair, but as a positive, courageous attempt to take hold of their own lives and make decisions about the future, instead of allowing others to dictate direction. Leaving home is very much a developmental process, the natural response of many young people to changing circumstances in their lives.

Far too often the popular conception of the homeless masks that fact. The problem of homelessness is viewed in the context of the personal and domestic difficulties of the individuals concerned. It is commonly held, therefore, that young people leave home because they have problems. This is true in some cases, but the reasons for moving out are as many as the individuals that make up the homeless group.

What is not clearly stressed is the fact that homelessness is a serious social problem, not because of the circumstances the individual is leaving behind, but because there are no structures in society that will allow those young people leaving home their basic human rights to shelter and independent living, regardless of their reasons for leaving. Many of the problems of ordinary young people who leave home and become homeless are due to the lack of housing provision for this group. For many young people, homelessness has as a consequence depression, loneliness and the inability to hold down employment. In general, homelessness deskills people for ordinary living. It is hard enough for young people with coping skills to survive. For those with additional personal and family difficulties, homelessness is a burden that can gradually wear them down.

The popular conception of the leaving-home process is a feeling that it is part of the impulsiveness of youth that always wants its own way. In this context, young people are seen to be naive, adrift, vulnerable and at risk. The young are said to leave home in search of adventure, because they want to, and are quite happy to put up with homelessness as part of this adventure. There is no doubt that there is an element among the young homeless that seeks to trade the sameness of the home area for the bright lights. London, in this context, is the place to be, because it is the capital, the centre of the country where everything happens.

However, by itself, such a view is seen to be a cynical distortion of the leaving-home process. Those working closely with the young homeless argue that there is an absence of any statement of how the young can legitimately leave home. The challenge, the excitement of a new life, are common elements in everyone's experience of leaving home. Homelessness is not an inevitable consequence of that process for many young people. That significant numbers do become homeless is due, in part, to the ambiguities and inconsistencies that surround young people in our society. These lead to what many workers describe as a basic denial of what should be a fundamental human right for everyone –to have a shelter and a security that can be termed home.

Current official and popular images of the young homeless are less fair to them. By leaving home not only are the young people taking a positive step in their development as young adults, but also for many such young people there is no alternative course of action. Their leaving home is a positive and courageous response to their 'home' circumstances.

The desire to escape family conflict
Problems within the family, real or imaginary, are often funda-mental to the process of leaving. Many young people feel they are the focus of discontent in the family and by moving out they will help to ease the disgruntlement in the home. Partly this has to do with the fact that the tension of being a teenager and a maturing adult can cause so much friction that relationships become unbearable. There is no doubt that the physical limitations of many households add to this tension. Many young people come from homes that are overcrowded, where conditions are stifling and inadequate. As the young grow up, they find that there is little opportunity for privacy and individuality and a move on becomes imperative.

Many would argue that this sort of move is little different to what countless youngsters do all the time. They leave home in a variety of ways—to go to college, to live with friends in digs, to be nearer a job, to take summer jobs at home or abroad. All this has as its purpose to distance the young person from the family as part of the natural, healthy, necessary process of becoming an adult. Most will want to and do maintain good relationships with home, relationships that are improved by moving away. There is no doubt that such young people form a substantial part of the homeless in Central London.

The increase in divorce
So many young people leave families where parents do not love each other and do not provide the role models from which a young

person can determine his or her priorities and shape the future. Many of these families will have broken up and the social trends of separation, divorce and remarriage often make home a place where it is impossible for the young person to survive. The Dartington Social Research Unit stated that by 1990 half the sixteen-year-olds in Britain will have experienced at least one change in their parental situation (Dartington Social Research Unit 1980).

The experience of *Clare* from Leeds, encountered in one of the Central London projects, is typical. She had left home because of the difficulties of living with her mother after her parents had divorced. She felt her mother had tried to compete with her and was jealous of her youth and freedom. She quite liked her father and his new wife, but felt that relationships would break down if she were to live permanently with them. She drifted initially into digs in Leeds, but had been frightened once too often by the requests of her landlady's boyfriend for money to pay for his drug habit. So she moved south with her boyfriend. At the time of our conversation she was living with three others in one room in a bed-and-breakfast hotel, and was finding the strain too great. She wanted to return to Leeds but was not sure if that were possible. The claustrophobia of her living conditions and the uncertainty of her future led her to feel low and very depressed.

The family scapegoat

Often the young people become the victims of the wishes of the adults in the family to start again and build a new life. A difficult, rebellious teenager can be awkward at the best of times, and when he or she is perceived as the threat to the newly-formed union, then the need for the scapegoat to be banished forever becomes overwhelming. On the other hand, it is sometimes the hostility of the new mother or new father that is so unbearable that the young person will 'choose' to leave rather than suffer any longer.

Such was the experience of two teenage lads from Ireland, one from Carlow in the south, the other from Belfast in the north.

Colum had fallen foul of his stepmother who, in his words, arrived one day with his father, who had left home for a while after the death of the mother of the family. Colum found himself being picked on continuously, though he admitted that he was not the easiest of fifteen-and-a-half-year-olds. Life was made even less bearable in Carlow by his girlfriend's parents who saw him as a complete undesirable for their daughter. He described himself as a bit of a tearaway who had found it hard to settle in a relatively small town that had provided little anonymity.

Colum had spent some time sleeping rough initially in Ireland before making the break and coming to London with his girlfriend to live in a squat. They felt they could live in London without prejudice and would have a better chance to live their lives anew. Sadly, Colum said that it had taken him three years to make sense of his scapegoating and he had suffered a great deal of anguish in that time, wondering why he had been so rejected.

Michael from Belfast told a similar story. He, too, had been picked on by his stepmother and forced out of home, a move made more urgent in his case because he had also fallen out with elements of one of the paramilitary groups in the province. He had first gone south to Dublin, but an experience one night, where he had been challenged verbally and physically about his political and religious views left him no option but to seek the anonymity that London offered.

Inadequacies in the family structure

The inability of family members to communicate with each other is another element in the leaving process for some young people.

Families are simply unable to comprehend the appeals of young people to be heard and because families cannot listen, they are bemused as to youth's need to be independent and to be accepted as people of worth in their own right.

More seriously, some young people come from families who are always living on the edge, barely able to cope as individuals and unable to live as members of a common home. Agency workers in London stress that many young people are simply not cared for, even in the most basic ways, by their families. Others stress the neglect of the individual that has left him or her with too much freedom, no structure, no boundaries to test out emerging awareness of what is right or wrong, good or bad.

At the same time, it is also clear that there are substantial numbers of young people in London whose freedom to choose the way of life they wish to live has been seriously limited by the relationships and circumstances of their family lives. Their abilities to cope have been undermined and they need varying levels of support to achieve their intended goals.

> *Rajesh* is one such lad. His family had sent him to India from his home in the Midlands at the age of eleven to study his religion for five years. As a result he felt he had lost out in terms of his secondary education. He had rowed with his parents on his return as the difficulties of his situation and the enormity of his educational loss had become clear. He initially had turned to his mosque for help. They had advised him to return home, but home had been unable to comprehend the depths of his dilemma. His English was poor and he felt trapped because of this. He saw no prospect of a job because of his lack of qualifications and this same factor, he felt, would prevent him going to college to study and to make up what he had lost. He had come to London in despair. He had contacted his family who had told him he could not return home until they had given him permission to do so. Rajesh was not optimistic that this permission would be forthcoming.

Although this case highlights a particular cultural dilemma that faces some young people, other young people have left homes where family supports have been poor at the best of times. In some cases these supports have never been present. Young people have suffered a great deal of neglect; some throughout their young lives from a very early age, others at a later stage in their development. There is no doubt that this group of young people has caused and is increasingly causing agency workers in London a great deal of concern.

The desire to find work

Economic realities, in particular the lack of employment, are significant factors in any analysis of the leaving-home process. The young often see themselves as a burden to their families and moving out is as much a wish to keep the family together as an escape from intolerable social and economic pressures. For many of these young people little more is needed than a place to live and the opportunity to make something of themselves. Their subsequent homelessness is due to the acute lack of housing provision and is not in any way a product of their own actions or inadequacies.

However, it is also true that education, or rather the lack of it, is an important factor. Without somewhere to live it is almost impossible for the young to gain employment. Without regular employment, it is likewise unlikely that they will find somewhere permanent to live. Into this equation must go the fact that the under-twenties are likely to be the least skilled group in the population, with a lower proportion of further education than any other group. Lack of qualifications means that their job prospects will be poor and for those who want to better themselves, regulations limit the amount of study that may be undertaken while on benefit. Youth Training Schemes are not altogether popular and are not seen as training that will lead to real employment.

Young people's expectations of the employment market in London are often grossly unrealistic. It is hard for them to accept that London may offer little more than their home areas for all the above reasons. Such work that is available is often unreliable and casual, likely to be withdrawn on the flimsiest of pretexts. Nonetheless, the lure of London's employment market is a significant factor in many young people's decisions to leave home.

Escape from abuse

There is no doubt that many young people leave home because they are unable to tolerate any longer the sexual abuse perpetrated by a parent or a close friend of the family. Many are also victims of a tremendous amount of physical violence, often from drunken parents, that may have been endured over a number of years. For others, there is a level of psychological abuse that makes them feel unloved and unwanted. It is a fact that some families are quite glad to get rid of their youngsters, no matter of what age, and agency workers tell many stories of parents abrogating all responsibility when contacted about a missing youngster.

There is also concern for those young people whose sexuality is an important factor in leaving home. The abuse that these young people suffer makes them unable to continue living either at home or in their home areas. Many feel it is better to come to the anonymity of London where being gay or lesbian is more acceptable. The isolation and abuse received in their home areas make the loneliness of London far more bearable, though agency workers still have concerns that despite all their efforts to accept them as they are, gay men and lesbians are still the object of abuse and scorn from fellow homeless young people.

Leaving care

For those young people who leave care or who are discharged from prisons or institutions, the leaving process has additional, more destructive elements. Some might argue that the process for these groups is different, but, essentially, the basic elements are the same. The desire to make one's own way, to gain employment, to escape overcrowding, abuse and the stifling conditions of the institution or home, are still strong motivating forces.

Between 30 and 40 per cent of young people using London's services for the homeless have been in care. Most are ill-equipped to cope and stand out clearly in projects as often the most disorganised and disconnected people around. Residential care has usually given them few coping skills and support from the statutory authorities, their legal parents, has often been at a minimum. It is alleged that some authorities send young people direct to London's homeless provisions because they have nothing for them in their local areas. Workers in the agencies feel strongly that this is a scandal that has to be brought out in the open. As a caring society, we fall down very badly with those to whom we have a legal obligation.

Some young people end up in care separated from their families, for no other reason than their family having nowhere to live. John Patten, then Minister at the Department of Health and Social

Security (DHSS), announced in June 1984 that in 1982 some 910 children in England and 65 in Wales had been taken into care for that reason.

In general, the representation of those who have been in care among the ranks of the single homeless is a cause for some concern. Fewer than one child in every hundred is taken into care. Yet a 1981 DHSS-sponsored survey found adults with a background in care making up 13 per cent of the single homeless. This figure grossly understates the present situation in London.

The process of leaving care is, for many, one of emotional and physical upheaval, often mirroring some of their movements while in care, and accompanied by the experience of living in inadequate and insecure accommodation. Homelessness is too often a consequence of that scenario. Many such young people find themselves out on the streets within a year of leaving care due to rent arrears, trouble with housing managers, or just the sheer inability to cope. Leaving care is a difficult enough experience without having to manage in addition with poor quality, hard-to-let accommodation and with minimal emotional support, so characteristic of the process for many young people. There is no doubt, and many workers argue this, that the provision of suitable housing is the single greatest obstacle to a young person leaving care overcoming the disadvantages of the child-care system.

In this context, independence-type programmes, that part of the leaving process that has as its aim to prepare the individual to cope with the future, come in for heavy criticism. Both the workers and the young people in the London agencies agree that too many of these programmes are started too late, offer too little, impose pressures that contribute to failure and are geared only to those who are likely to succeed. The general complaint is that the system appears to be more of a controlling mechanism to help authorities cope with difficult and rebellious teenagers, than a genuine aid towards independent living.

What is good for the authority is a factor which a young person in care or in an institution has to take into account when the time comes to move on. It is no wonder that agencies point to this group of homeless young people as the most difficult to cope with. Workers quote as a particular example the problems of those in prison. The tendency has been over the years to give custodial sentences to those convicted of offences who come from poor home conditions or who are homeless. Far from helping the individual, this has led to overcrowding in prisons and increased vulnerability to homelessness on release.

There is no doubt that those leaving care or institutions have particular difficulties to overcome. Their vulnerability to homelessness is a matter of great concern and it will continue to be so. The risk will only begin to be reduced when those who are legally responsible for such young people have an awareness and an understanding of the leaving process that will enable them to make significant changes in the care programmes of such young people and the training of those who are charged with implementing them.

Conclusion

Leaving home is a reality that will not go away. It marks the transition from adolescence to young adulthood and is a significant time in everyone's life. It is essential that this happens for being an adult is defined as being outside and apart from one's parents. The problem is that leaving home is not understood as a reality, hence the ambiguity that Barbara Saunders highlights in the quote that opened this chapter. As a consequence, young people expect it to be difficult to leave home and many leave far later than they really want to. There is no doubt that some young women especially tolerate quite difficult and distressing situations at home because of the lack of suitable alternatives.

Little is done, on the other hand, to educate young people to the realities surrounding leaving home. It ought not to be left solely to the last months of school as this distorts its importance in a young person's life. All our lives are, in part, a history of leaving, with particular stress in our early years on the process of moving away from the family—initially to school, primary and secondary, then out to work or further education and ultimately to our own home and the creation of a new family. Greater awareness of these processes is an essential aspect in overcoming the issues that homelessness presents in society. Unfortunately, part of the difficulty has to do with the notion that anyone who does anything positive in this area is encouraging young people to leave home. Until this attitude can be changed the fundamental issues of leaving home will continue to be glossed over.

2 The background to the problem

'The fate of the street generation is inseparable from the uncertain future of cities. Bursting or decaying, they were never built with the needs of children in mind. Today, the notion of man as the measure of all things has long vanished from urban life and huge urban agglomerations have become increasingly inhuman and unmanageable. Beyond a certain point their problems multiply faster than the means of solving them. Administration becomes remote from the people it is meant to serve. Street children are poignant evidence of this reality.' (Susanna Agnelli, *Street Children. A Growing Urban Tragedy.*)

The size of the problem

It is commonly held that the numbers of the young homeless in London are rising significantly, but it is hard to prove this with effective statistics. There are no accurate data and the evidence that does exist is largely anecdotal and incomplete. It has been consistently argued, however, that the statistics that do exist underestimate very substantially the scale and complexity of actual homelessness.

The study by John Greve and his team on homelessness in London gave three reasons for this (Greve 1985). Local authorities record as homeless only those categorised as priority cases according to the 1977 Housing Act (see pages 25-6), but Greve felt that only about half of those who could be classed as priority bothered to apply. He argued that many homeless would not approach housing departments, simply because they felt it would be a waste of time to do so. Third, Greve's team said that there was a serious under-reporting of homelessness by local authorities in inner London where the numbers were highest.

Some of the agencies that deal with homeless young people in London do record faithfully the numbers of those using their services and their reasons for coming to the capital, but these are very much the exception. A great number of the agencies keep no figures at all, most because they have neither the time nor the facilities to carry out accurate recording. Some agencies refuse to

do so because they believe that they should not intrude into the
lives of the young people. They work on the principle that allows
the individual to offer as much or as little information as he or
she wishes.

This latter view is important. There is no doubt that some homeless young people are very cautious and suspicious of authority.
They shy away from anything that smacks of bureaucracy for fear
that anything written down could be used to cause them or their
friends pain or distress. It can take a lot of time and effort to win
over these young people to the point where they are willing to
impart information. Most agencies are not geared structurally or
financially to carry out such a task.

With no umbrella body to co-ordinate research, the scale and
complexity of those leaving home, running away or at risk in
Central London is extremely difficult to record accurately and in
a way that prevents double counting. The young who come into
London are handled by a number of agencies over a period of days,
weeks or even months and there is no way definitive numbers
can be established. However, few of those who work in the field
would argue with Shelter's assertion of 80,000 young homeless
nationally and the Advisory Service for Squatters' estimate of
30–35,000 young squatters in London between the ages of twenty
and thirty.

There is no doubt that the growth of squatting as a major
housing option for the young makes them a difficult group to
quantify. John Greve's report highlighted the growth of this form
of housing in Southwark from May 1981 to April 1985. Squats
increased from 150 to 1,219 in the borough in that period—a
growth of one squat a day. The Greater London Council (GLC)
quoted the figure of 30,000 in squats in 1985 (Livingstone 1985)
and added that the numbers sleeping rough or in unsatisfactory
temporary accommodation in London were estimated at well over
20,000 by councils and voluntary agencies, though the actual totals
of the single and homeless, in the opinion of the GLC, had to
be substantially higher.

Many young people have little option but to sleep out and this
factor is yet another obstacle to gathering accurate data. In 1985–86,
1,500 were estimated as living on the streets of Camden and
Labour councillors claimed in January 1987 that between 25,000
and 40,000 were living rough in the London area (Jones 1987). All
workers would agree that it is impossible to make accurate assess-

ments. Greve's team said that significant numbers were involved in sleeping out while admitting that as a group they were very hard to quantify. This is especially true for the young. More than any other group they are very hard to pin down and they are often not as visible to outreach groups as certain other age groups sleeping rough.

The indicators
With problems in collecting reliable data on the use of the services available and no co-ordinating body with the resources to oversee the research, other indicators have to be looked to in order to gain some idea of how serious is the problem of the young single homeless in London.

Juveniles
Juveniles, that is those seventeen years of age and under, are a particularly difficult group to quantify. Because of their age and their status in law (those under 16 have no right to be away from home), juveniles may often lie about their dates of birth in order to gain entry into a project and benefit from the support it can offer. Others fear being returned to their homes and may steer well clear of any of the agencies who deal with the homeless. Few will carry identification and, despite that, agencies will not initially deny support.

Perhaps some indication of the number of juveniles who are away from home and possibly at risk in London can be seen from the statistics of the Metropolitan Police. In 1986, 478 boys and 419 girls under fourteen years of age were reported missing. Forty-seven boys and 24 girls were not found. Of those between the ages of fourteen and seventeen, 813 boys and 1,167 girls were reported missing and 54 boys and 63 girls were not found. Those not found represent 6.5 per cent of the total reported. Erica De'Ath of the Children's Society estimates that between 75,000 and 85,000 children were reported missing nationally to the police in 1985 (De'Ath 1987). Based on London's percentages, between 4,800 and 5,500 of them would not be found. Added to these figures are the numbers of those who are reported missing to the police and are found within a short period. Their report forms are not kept, but the Metropolitan Police estimate around 20,000 such young people were reported in 1986. Then there are those who go missing and are never reported by parents or those responsible. Workers in

London's agencies attest the fact that this situation is not as uncommon as one would like to believe.

Attached to Vine Street Police Station in Soho is a squad of six policemen and policewomen, called the Juvenile Protection Bureau. Their role is to protect juveniles from the bright lights and attractions of the Central London area. The size of the squad and the time allocated to their duties limit the work that they can do. Between March 1986 and May 1987 the team picked up 201 juveniles who were deemed to be at risk, the youngest of whom was four years of age. In that time 168 arrests were made of adults for sexual offences with young people. However, the team is clear that the numbers of those picked up as at risk is directly related to the amount of time they are able to spend on the streets. So much of their time is spent in the office, on the phone, or waiting for a responsible adult to arrive so a young person can be questioned. They are sure that more young people would be helped in this way if officers could spend much more time on the streets.

Between January and August 1987 Euston Railway police had a direct involvement with 99 juveniles between the ages of nine and seventeen. Seventy were males and 29 females, the majority aged between twelve and sixteen. Most had been missing from home for a day or so. Forty-one per cent were runaways from local authority care. Ten per cent had committed some offence for which they had been cautioned. Thirty-six per cent came from London, the South East and the Home Counties, with 28 per cent from the Midlands, 14 per cent from Scotland and the North and 18 per cent from the North East and North West.

The Railway police were clear that this represented only the tip of the iceberg, being those youngsters whose demeanour or behaviour had made it clear that they had wanted to be picked up. They felt that many more such young people pass through Euston without becoming involved with the police. The Police and Criminal Evidence Act 1984 means that officers have to be more sure of their grounds before picking up a young person on suspicion that they might be in difficulties. In addition, the Railway police felt that the publicity surrounding runaways over the years and, more recently, the attempts of the Metropolitan Police to curb prostitution in the Euston and Kings Cross areas had meant that the problem of the young alone and at risk was not so visible. However, the Railway police were adamant that the problem had not gone away.

Other indicators give glimpses of the extent of the difficulties and back up this assertion that the problem has not gone away.

Threshold, a housing advice group for the single homeless and couples without children, carried out a survey of all those under twenty-six years of age who approached their centre in Wandsworth for advice between October 1986 and March 1987. Thirty-eight were between the ages of sixteen and seventeen, 11 per cent of the total. One in three of all their callers had nowhere to stay for the night (Sutton 1987).

Off Centre, a counselling and advice service in Hackney, deals with around 45 under-sixteen-year-olds a year and in 1986 gave a service to 195 sixteen- to eighteen-year-olds.

Railway police in Victoria felt that the ages of those sleeping out were falling, but that the numbers of those under seventeen had not increased over the past twelve to fourteen years.

However, all these figures can do is give glimpses of the problem. Workers argue consistently that there are substantial numbers of juveniles homeless and at risk in London, a fact substantiated by the young people in the projects. The feeling is that those who attract the attention of the statutory and voluntary services are the minority. The majority, it is said, avoid such services because of their age and the feeling that they will not be given the help they require. Until a proper monitoring system can be set up, such glimpses will be the only way of recording the numbers of juveniles who are homeless in the capital.

Older teenagers
A little more clarity is available when looking at the numbers of older teenagers. Over-sixteens are at least legally allowed to leave home with their parents' consent. Without this consent their position is less clear. However, it seems discretion is used by police in returning seventeen-year-olds, who are adults according to criminal law, or young people who have not committed an offence. Still most young people, sixteen years of age and over, will be dealt with by the agencies as legally away from home unless there is clear evidence to the contrary.

Figures, however, must still be taken cautiously. Young people move around the agencies in London, though the latter do try to prevent any doubling up of services. In 1985, the *Soho Project* reported dealing with 2,000 young people between the ages of sixteen and twenty-five. Some of these would have come via the

emergency night shelter of the agency, *Centrepoint*, which has a
formal agreement to send a certain number of the night-shelter
clients there each day. Centrepoint itself saw 1,787 young people
in its night shelter in 1986, a drop of about 15 per cent on the
figures from the previous year. On the other hand, the *Piccadilly
Advice Centre* saw an increase of 31.8 per cent in those coming to
the centre in 1985/86, up from 16,057 in 1984/85 to 21,170. The *New
Horizon Day Centre* sees around 3,000 young people, twenty-one
years of age and under, each year, and the *Alone in London Advice
and Counselling Centre* (ALS) saw 443 new clients in 1985/86, a
marginal increase from 1984/85, and that despite difficulties with
premises that meant they could only be fully operational from the
September. Just under 200 of this group were seventeen years old
or younger. ALS receive a number of referrals direct from Centrepoint and in general there would be a certain amount of doubling
up in statistical terms between all the above agencies.

There are also a number of smaller agencies who record information about the young people using their services. The *Irish
Centre* in Camden dealt with 375 young Irish people under
eighteen years of age and a further 1,296 between the ages of
eighteen and twenty-five in 1986. *Threshold's* statistics showed that
57 per cent of all callers were aged twenty-five or under during
their survey period, while *Off Centre* in Hackney saw 118 young
people in the same age group in 1986. The *Passage* day centre in
Victoria, which sees a good number, mainly older people, of those
sleeping rough or in squats, gave formal advice to over 200 young
people under twenty-five years of age in 1986/87, though workers
felt that double that number came for advice without reaching
the stage where the request was formally recorded. In a report
in 1984 the *Hackney Short Life Users Group* showed 67 per cent of
those applying for accommodation were between the ages of
sixteen and twenty-four.

Without a proper system of recording it is difficult to make sense
of all these figures. All those working in the field would argue
that they represent only the tip of the iceberg and many are
adamant that the word on the streets is that many young people
do not use the agencies at all. All these factors have to be taken
into account and perhaps a proposed study by the Institute of
Community Studies about the young homeless in Hackney will
come up with a blueprint that will enable statistics to be kept that
record accurately the nature and scale of the problem.

The source of the problem

It is clear from the figures that are available that the number of young single people homeless in London is substantial with no indication that it is decreasing.

The reasons for the crisis are related to the rights of these people under current housing legislation, the shortage and cost of

housing in the capital and the increase in demand for this type
of housing by sections of society who are considered to be of
higher priority than young single people.

The shortage of housing
Workers point to the acute lack of housing provision for the young
homeless as the fundamental reason why so many of them have
to live rough or in squats. Essentially, this is a reflection on the
crisis in London's housing.

The extent of the crisis
The 1986 regional strategy statement by the Housing Corporation
underlines the extent of the crisis (The Housing Corporation 1986).

Hackney, with the worst overall deprivation of any local authority
in England, has massive overcrowding with 6,200 households
living at more than one person to a room. Because of the rise of
priority homeless in the borough, only a limited response is possible for the single homeless.

Camden's shortfall of dwellings against households is 13,000.
Existing stock is deteriorating. Over 10,000 dwellings are unfit and
require replacement and 35 per cent of the housing stock in the
borough is unsatisfactory. Over 5,500 households approached the
council as homeless in 1984/85—an understatement of the real
need. About 7,000 single people are living permanently in hostels
or hotels.

In *Islington,* 20 per cent of the dwellings in the borough are
statutorily unfit for habitation and in *Hammersmith and Fulham,*
the borough suffers the third highest proportion of unfit dwellings
in London at 16.4 per cent of its stock. A similar proportion lacks
amenities and requires repairs. *Kensington and Chelsea* is the most
densely populated borough in London, ranking third in terms of
lack of amenities and fifth in terms of overcrowding among the
English District and Metropolitan Councils.

Private rented accommodation in London has fallen by 7 per
cent since 1981 and new lettings to council tenants have dropped
by more than 12 per cent over the same period. Since the mid-
seventies the number of dwellings in management by London
councils has fallen by 75 per cent. This situation is unlikely to be
improved given existing policies on the tenants' right to buy rented
property and cuts in Government provision for housing capital
spending by more than three-quarters in real terms since 1979/80.

Vacant properties

Little has been done to bring into use the large number of properties standing empty in the private sector, while the growth of sub-standard bed-and-breakfast hotels charging the maximum rates possible puts severe pressure on local authority budgets and contributes nothing to permanent provision. Shelter has estimated that two-thirds of London's vacant property is owned privately, with the largest number in the Westminster area, ironically the borough where the single homeless gather (McKechnie 1987). An article in the *London Daily News* in April 1987 quoted 94,000 private and 27,000 council properties as vacant in London (Glancey 1987). Kensington and Chelsea are the worst culprits with nearly 9,000 homes empty in the private sector and 500 in the public. Westminster has 7,000 vacant private houses and only 3 per cent of its public stock.

Glancey listed four main factors that contributed to the existence of empty properties: the amount of time it took to complete a private sale, the huge backlog of major repairs needed by London's housing stock, the number of houses waiting for planning permission for conversion, and finally the speculation of owners waiting to cash in on what Glancey called 'London's property price casino'.

The condition of housing stock

A DHSS report in 1976 said then that the provision of single-person accommodation in London had to be seen in the context of a continuing acute housing shortage. The report of John Greve and his team (Greve 1985) made it clear that this trend was continuing. They found that much of London's housing stock was in poor condition, made worse because of owners' neglect, restrictions on public spending and inadequate expenditure on maintenance, improvement and rehabilitation. All this they found exacerbated the problems of shortage and access and led to overcrowding in some areas and among particular groups.

A survey by the Department of Environment, reporting in Parliament in January 1987 on the conditions of multiple-occupation housing in England and Wales, painted a distressing picture. Seventy-five per cent of tenants lived in one small room of less than 15 square metres. Damp and condensation were common and 20 per cent of households had a lack of proper facilities for preparing and storing food and no toilet. Half the houses surveyed needed repair and upgrading costing over £10,000 and a further

10 per cent needed work costing £25,000. Most of all, landlords either did not do repairs, or where they did, did not do them properly or quickly enough. It is no wonder then that so many households become homeless, especially in London.

The public v. *the private sector*
This trend in the shortage of housing has been well documented. Greve and his team warned, however, that the shortage of council housing could lead to patterns of homelessness in the public sector comparable to those long familiar in the private sector (Greve 1985). This is perhaps one reason why in 1986 London recorded its highest ever figures of households registered on housing waiting lists—272,000 (McKechnie 1987)—and why Maurice Barnes of the Association of London Authorities could state in April 1987 that if nothing were done in the following eighteen months, there would be more homeless families than bed-and-breakfast spaces in London and many people would be forced on to the streets (Wolmar 1987).

There is also the argument that forces outside the control of authorities will continue to fuel London's crisis. This says that the trend of people to move into cities is an irreversible one and a Gallup poll commissioned by the International Year of Shelter for the Homeless showed sixteen- to twenty-five-year-olds wanted higher spending on shelter in the South of England (Seabrooke 1987).

Shelter has pointed out that investment in housing by both public and private sectors is 17 per cent less now than it was twenty years ago, and the effects have fallen hardest on those who use rented accommodation, especially the single homeless (McKechnie 1987). Even those who have rented accommodation are finding it hard to cope. Cuts in housing benefits are leading to more rent arrears and subsequent evictions. With landlords presently being able to let for as little as one year at a time and tenants needing about three months to get a fair rent registered, security of tenure for many is a mere nine months. Although assured tenancies are to be made easier to get, they will offer security to tenants only for as long as they can pay whatever rent is demanded, no matter how high. It is hard to escape the conclusion that housing will only be available for the wealthy and with house building dropping and repairs/improvement grants decreasing, the outlook is not a happy one for the young homeless.

The trends

The report of the GLC in 1985 (Livingstone 1985) made it clear that London's housing problem was a growing one and that there was no evidence to suggest that it would not continue to grow. Greve and his team backed up that assertion. They stated that homelessness has been a growing problem in London since 1947, apart from the mid-fifties and the years 1975–77. They do point out, however, that while the general trend was upwards, the pace of growth had varied and, in the mid-seventies, even began to slow down. Since 1985 there has been a resurgence in the pace of increase while the numbers of lettings made to the waiting list by the boroughs and the GLC have fallen since 1977/78 (Greve 1985, 1986). All this has to be seen in the context of the expansion of owner occupation and the dramatic rise in house prices in the capital.

The official response to the crisis

There is no doubt that the effects of the housing shortage are coming home to those in government. A report of the Association of Conservative District Councils in March 1987 (Deer 1987) said that the number of families presenting themselves as homeless was so great that radical steps, such as the buying of caravans, would have to be taken to find them places to live. There are calls to require councils to list properties vacant for six months or more. Councils, it is argued, should be required to state how many properties in their borough are empty, how long they have been empty, why they are empty and whether they have squatters or not.

Nicholas Ridley, the Environment Secretary, condemned the levels of empty properties in March 1987 and urged that a 'home-steading' scheme be adopted whereby run-down properties would be released to applicants for renovation as part of an ownership deal. He said that he had some sympathy for the view that this scheme should apply to any property vacant for six months and that councils should be forced to sell after that time (Pienaar 1987).

Councils, however, are not faced with any easy solutions to the problem. Spending less on bed-and-breakfast accommodation and putting the money saved into repairing and renovating run-down housing, so providing permanent accommodation, is not as straightforward as it sounds. Vacant properties take time to reno-vate and individually are often part of a wider plan for housing

in the borough, dependent on other forces outside the council.
Secondly, the priority homeless have, legally, to be housed immediately. As a report in the *Sunday Times* in January 1987 pointed
out, this is why anomalies exist. Hackney spends £4 million a year
on bed and breakfast, yet has not the money to house its 700
homeless families in its 3,752 empty council properties. It has 5.5
per cent of rent arrears, 16 per cent of collectable income, and an
annual repair bill of £20.75 million for its 40,000 homes. Repair
and re-let takes an average of six months. On the other hand,
Wandsworth spends £12 million on the same number of houses,
takes three weeks to repair and re-let, yet still had, in January 1987,
182 families in bed and breakfast (Jacobs 1987).

Nicholas Ridley urged the homeless in March 1987 to go where
there was a home rather than sleep rough in London. He said
it was 'crass and incompetent not to realise that it is better to find
a home where there is one empty than sleep out on the pavement
when you do not have to' (Pienaar 1987).

In the same month, Westminster Council told 40 bed-and-breakfast hotels in Bayswater to evict homeless families, decreeing it
illegal for them to house such groups. It also made it clear that
other councils would be told to stop dumping the homeless in
Westminster and to accommodate them themselves, a practice
since taken up by a number of other boroughs (Leonard 1987).

The Housing Corporation in its annual report has made it clear
that it will cease to make the refurbishment of existing stock a
priority in some London boroughs and in fact says that it will
become unachievable on all but an occasional basis. The rising
price of property in London and the needs of the elderly and the
homeless will put an impossible strain on their resources. Large-
scale development will also have to be curtailed—a bleak prospect
for those most at need.

The perception of homelessness as a localised phenomenon has
not helped the particular, national problems faced by London.
Greve pointed out that London's share of capital investment had
been reduced and the weighting of the indicators in the General
Needs Index (used by the Department of Environment to allocate
housing resources to local authorities) tended to disadvantage the
capital. He felt that this was because the kind of housing problems
by which London is most severely affected did not receive adequate recognition in the GNI (Greve 1985).

This lack of recognition goes further. David Brandon pointed out in 1980 that in contrast to the growth of the welfare state over the previous seventy years, the homeless section of society had experienced a contraction in statutory provision and a growing development in the work of voluntary organisations (Brandon *et al* 1980). The argument about homelessness as a local problem applies here, but there are other, more fundamental effects. There is no doubt that the difficulties that face voluntary groups in their efforts to find revenue funding seriously inhibit voluntary effort, innovation and expansion and lead to instability in project management.

The eyes of the law
Workers argue that the 1977 and 1985 Housing Acts must be amended if any possibility is to exist to house the young homeless. At present, the Acts state that someone is homeless if he or she, together with anyone who normally resides with him or her, has no accommodation which he or she is entitled to occupy, or cannot secure entry into such accommodation. A person is threatened with homelessness if he or she is likely to become homeless in twenty-eight days.

However, the Acts then determine that three other factors must be established if someone is to be eligible for housing and it is here that differences of opinion abound. The Acts talk of those in 'priority need' but do not include the young unless they are 'vulnerable'. Second, the homeless must have a local connection and those who live away from home, especially in institutions, have great difficulty here. Third, a person must not be intentionally homeless, that is, he or she must not do something deliberately or fail to do it, as a consequence of which accommodation is lost. This clause does not include acts or omissions done in good faith. Nonetheless, as many have pointed out, this excludes those who are discharged from institutions of all types, those living with friends or relatives in crowded conditions, those in crash pads, reception centres, derelict buildings, unlicensed squats, hotels, lodging houses, cheap hotels and boarding houses.

In general, workers, and those who write about homelessness, are very critical of the way in which these Acts are implemented. Greve and his team felt that the root cause of the anomalies lay in the differentiation the Acts made on social and personal criteria rather than on the basis of the objective housing circumstances of the individual. They argued that the philosophy and approach of the 1977 Act was inherently discriminatory and they felt it prevented a comprehensive look at housing needs as expressed in homelessness. The Act encouraged squatting by its discrimination of the single homeless and those from ethnic minority groups in particular.

Others have argued for a change in the Vagrancy Acts of 1824 and 1933 and the difficulties they present for the young to receive financial help (Brandon *et al* 1980). Some workers argue for these Acts to be repealed so that homelessness is no longer considered a crime and for greater liaison between the police, the homeless and the statutory and voluntary agencies.

The most consistent and serious criticism of the 1977 and 1985 Housing Acts is the way in which they are interpreted in relation to the young, despite evidence of the social effects of their vulnerability. As early as 1982, statistics from the Housing Advice Switchboard in London showed 18 per cent of all enquiries came from sixteen- to eighteen-year-olds. Forty-four per cent of those had nowhere to sleep on the night they consulted the agency. There is no doubt that some of those would have been open to sexual and financial exploitation, but few would have been acceptable as vulnerable to local authorities (Hilditch 1982). These figures bear comparison with those quoted earlier from Threshold and, given the earlier provisos about statistics, show that the situation in London is far from improving.

The National Association for the Care and Resettlement of Offenders (NACRO) has argued that all homeless young people aged between sixteen and seventeen should be declared a priority and it has consistently proposed that the vulnerability clause be extended to include the young who are at risk of offending or re-offending. It would like to see hostel residents considered as having a local connection in the area of the hostel, unless it is clearly established that they have one in another authority's area. It also wants the law changed so that a young person under eighteen years of age, at present legally a minor, can be granted a tenancy (NACRO 1981).

In general, the Acts exclude the majority of single people and couples without children. Many workers feel that, unless this fundamental issue is looked at, little can be done to resolve some of the problems of single homelessness.

The rising cost of housing

Perhaps the most critical contributing factor to youth homelessness
has been the rising cost of housing and its scarcity in areas where
employment is available. Rents have risen consistently since the
war as a percentage of average earnings and the private rented
sector has correspondingly diminished. For such places that are
available the young are frozen out either because the emphasis
is put on family accommodation, or where single accommodation
is available, the deposit alone immediately disqualifies them.

The growing demand for housing

There are other forces at work that put pressure on rented housing
in London and which relegate the young to the bottom of the
queue.

More and more of those with mortgages are having to hand back
their houses to building societies. The growth in divorce means
that around 30,000 divorced people a year from owner-occupied
homes will be looking for rented accommodation and they will
compete with the 25,000 extra households already living in rented
accommodation when they were divorced. The proportion of the
elderly in society has increased and will continue to do so. The
age at which people marry has fallen and more couples are living
together without marrying. Thus the demand for smaller units
of accommodation has increased. Yet, in 1986, local authorities
started to build only 31,800 homes in total (Lipsey 1987). Pressures
are increasing on the young to leave home and there is an
increasing number who are being forced to do so.

The recent closures of large-scale hostels in London and the
general shift away from residential care to a care-in-the-community
policy has put greater stress on the sort of accommodation that
might have been available to the young single homeless. The eight-
week rule that decrees that the DHSS will not bear the cost of
accommodation, for those who are under twenty-six years of age,
in any given area, for more than eight weeks, reduces the slight
chance the young might have of finding both work and accommodation in London.

One of the trends that is causing serious concern to workers
in the agencies is the growing band, particularly of young people,
who are suffering from severe mental illness. Malcolm Weller, a
doctor at Friern Barnet, carried out a survey in London of 100
homeless men and women on Christmas Eve 1986. He found

42 per cent actively psychotic, suffering from delusions and hallu-
cinations, compared to 9 per cent mentally ill in a similar survey
in 1985. Thirty per cent had definite or probable schizophrenia
compared to one in 3–4,000 in the general population. Over half
those interviewed had slept out in the open the night before
(Snellgrove 1987). It is not clear what percentage were of the
younger age group, but the evidence of the West-End agencies
suggests that they would not be under-represented. In the long
term the demand to care for and house these groups will grow.

The cost of homelessness
The costs of homelessness are enormous in London and run into
millions. Statistics from the Chartered Institute (CIPFA 1986)
showed that almost £40 million was spent on homelessness by
those London boroughs who replied to their enquiries, with
Camden, Tower Hamlets and Brent the biggest spenders. Fifty per
cent of the people housed were in bed and breakfast with a further
19 per cent in hostels. Estimates are that bed and breakfast cost
London boroughs over £100 million in 1987 (Stein 1987). To keep
a family of four in a hotel costs £21,000 a year. An average cost
to local authorities at present is £17 per bed space per night in
a London hotel.

All this poses problems for the young. The maximum allowance
for board and lodging is currently £70 per week. The meals allowance in this is £29.40 per week. That leaves £40.60, or £5.80 per
day, to find somewhere to live. Many young people have to supplement this with allowances given for personal requisites and
laundry (£15 per week) to try to find somewhere to live. Even then,
they quite often have to make a choice between going hungry or
having a bed for the night. Quite often they follow a pattern of
a few nights inside and a few sleeping out so that they can balance
their budgets.

Official government figures in January 1987 showed that housing
the homeless in bed and breakfast costs almost double the amount
needed to buy and renovate empty properties. Buying and renovating properties would cost the taxpayer around £5,500 a year
in interest charges and maintenance. New homes would cost
£7,000 a year. On average bed and breakfast costs £10,950 a year
(Hencke 1987). SHAC estimates that it costs £4,140 a year to keep
a single person in board and lodging. This compares with a first-

year cost of £6,588 to build a self-contained, one-person flat, with costs declining in subsequent years (Locks 1987).

There is no doubt that present policies towards the homeless need revising. Workers argue that costs alone require such a revision. It is estimated that the monies spent in London on providing unsatisfactory accommodation could have built 12,000 new homes (Stein 1987). Some of the existing regulations are open to abuse and there are many examples of unscrupulous hotel owners charging councils more than twice their currrent bed-and-breakfast rate. One such example was exposed in January 1987 in three hotels owned by a commercial group. Ordinary visitors were charged between £8 and £15 per night, while council tenants had to pay between £17.50 and £34, with often six homeless people crowded into one room (Tirbutt 1987). It is no wonder that estimates of costs to house the homeless in London are expected to rise still further.

Conclusion

In general, strategies to help the homeless largely exclude those who are young and single. There is a tendency to blame them for being layabouts or scroungers and for officialdom to pass the buck in relation to their needs. Government departments have often told these young people that their hands are tied despite their wish to help. The only advice that is given to so many is to return home to those situations in which many have originally found it impossible to survive.

Young people complain that officialdom seems not to care. It does not seem to understand that living in a squalid bed and breakfast, sometimes four to a room, is no substitute for having one's own place. Even the money given out to survive in that level of accommodation is insufficient. Voluntary agencies do not escape criticism. Some of the campaigning on behalf of the homeless is hard to understand. Arguing that nothing ought to be done for the homeless unless carried out by government, pressing for existing places to be closed down without a guarantee that new ones will open, seems to be somewhat misguided and idealistic. Young people complain that agencies often patronise them and refuse to believe that they are capable of making their own decisions. Yet some of those same agencies are very quick to reject them if they make a mess of things.

There are some suggestions that local authorities are attempting to bring Social Services and Housing Departments together to offer a better service to the needy. But apart from this ray of hope, the trends are not encouraging. With no effective method of quantifying need and little chance that the housing situation will improve, there is little chance of tackling the source of the problems facing the young homeless. They are bound to suffer still more. The study of David Brandon and his team in the mid-seventies questioned whether what was being done then for London's young homeless was effective. They said there was a need for social work, psychotherapy and counselling to treat emotional deprivation and called, even at that time, for a 'major social intervention' rather than the 'specific individualised solutions of the agencies' (Brandon *et al* 1980).

The comments of Lord Scarman, at the opening of the International Year of Shelter for the Homeless, showed that little had changed in the years following Brandon's report. Indeed he was far more despondent. He said that a decline to a new 'Fagin's London' was inevitable unless we as a society made a determined effort to put a stop to it now. He talked of homelessness 'disintegrating and destroying human personality' and warned that, as the condition of world-wide homelessness and the threat to our own housing stock showed, 'civilisation would be in peril' if homelessness was not tackled (Andrews 1987).

3 The reality

'Being homeless is rotten. In a world of statistics and social analysis, that is sometimes overlooked . . . For a start you are not needed by anyone . . . You have nowhere to go and nothing to do except get through the day and night. You wander amidst bustling crowds of clean, well-fed and burly people . . . You have little money, no friends, and almost no content to your life save to keep warm in the libraries or queue up for your benefit at the Social Security. Worst of all you are alone and that brings with it an increasing sense of isolation.' (Alaistair and Gabrielle Cox, *Borderlines: A Partial View of Detached Work with Homeless Young People.*)

The effects of homelessness

Homelessness is sadly becoming a way of life for whole generations of young people. This causes great concern to all of those who work with them.

The young are optimists, however, and Brandon's team found that there were positive experiences related to being homeless in Central London (Brandon *et al* 1980). There was 'the excitement of meeting dossers; the challenge of surviving and learning new social skills like begging; the freedom of being away from the parental home; the lights and sights of London and being at the centre of things'. The benefits of homeless accommodation were often highly rated by Brandon's subjects.

But, there was a negative side, too—loneliness, deprivation, sleeping rough, walking the streets feeling cold, hungry, down and out and inadequate, the shame of asking for help, the confusion and hostility of London, the suspicion of others who were homeless and the cost of food and accommodation.

Brandon felt that for many the homeless community in the West End was the closest to a family that many young people had had. However, this community could not supplement the lack of guaranteed personal support and material help given by so many families to their young when they first leave home. Homelessness creates a dislocated and alienated group of young people who are severed from their own community and roots.

Lord Scarman was just as insistent on the evil effects of homelessness. He saw it as providing a breeding ground for crime, marital breakdown, child abuse and neglect (Andrews 1987).

As long ago as 1970, a study by Joy Holloway (quoted by Brandon (Brandon *et al* 1980)) of twenty-five homeless men under thirty years of age in Leeds, suggested that 80 per cent had an obvious mental disorder, even though only five had ever seen a psychiatrist. Half had had prison sentences, and all but six had had some trouble with the police as adults.

Even those who have somewhere to live are not free from risk. Families who have had to wait eighteen months in bed and breakfast before being housed have suffered severe stress. Women and children are most at risk because of the length of time they have to spend indoors.

The need for money
The young homeless list a number of issues when they describe the difficulties they have in day-to-day survival. Getting money to live is the priority and this is required basically for four items—food, lodging, clothes and cigarettes.

Obtaining money
In addition to that obtained from the DHSS, most obtain money in a variety of ways. Some receive hand-outs from the agencies, around £1.50 to £2 on a daily basis, if they have no other immediate source of income, though not every agency is able to offer such a service. Most of those young homeless talked to admitted to buying cigarettes with that money. Cigarettes are an important requisite in the daily grind on the basis that they help young people to survive and are a calming influence. Many prefer to buy them and go without anything to eat during the day if they can get something to eat either mornings or evenings.

For many young homeless there is little option but to resort to other ways of getting money. Some admit to begging and, though they resent having to do so, 'living on charity' one said, they could sometimes make up to £10 on a good day. Often this is spent immediately on a good meal and a drink. So many have stressed the importance that young people place on living for today and letting tomorrow take care of itself. As one put it, in the middle of a casual conversation, 'Tomorrow is when you wake up. We live from day to day. If we had thought about tomorrow, we would not have survived.'

However, not all the young homeless have that approach. Some do make great efforts to save money to buy decent clothing and footwear for job interviews. One talked of being unable to take up a sporting option at a day centre because he did not have the required trainers. He had enough money to buy them, but felt he had to spend it on a pair of shoes for a job interview in the days following. The fact that his being of no fixed abode would probably work against him in the interview did not deter this young man from getting what he saw as his priorities right.

Making a claim
Making a successful claim is the most difficult problem the young homeless face. The fact that different Social Security offices have different identity requirements is irksome, but being passed from one office to another is very frustrating and the cause of a great deal of anger amongst the young. Many have highlighted the strain in trying to live on £29 for three weeks or more while waiting for a claim to be established. It is very hard to survive. One put his hand in his pocket and produced two £1 coins. This, he said, was all he had to live on until his claim was ratified. He had no idea when that would be. He had been told to return to the DHSS office within two days, but had not been given assurances that his claim would have been processed by then.

The problem of obtaining money from the DHSS when you are young and homeless is a major issue in London. The most consistent and strongly held feelings expressed by both workers in the agencies and the young people related to the approach of the DHSS offices and the attitudes of the staff in them. These offices are often described as violent places where the young homeless are treated as little better than common criminals asking for that which they are not entitled to. The complaints about these offices are legion. Staff are said to be rude, inconsistent and downright unhelpful more often than not. Managers, it is alleged, make up the rules as they go along and the system is run, it is said, to keep the young ignorant and to cheat them out of that which is their right.

Many groups exist to monitor the performance of these offices and to intervene when disputes arise. They have evidence of offices treating identical cases in completely opposing ways. Even where dialogue is established with managers, problems consistently arise. These are due more often than not to the inexperience of the DHSS staff, their lack of training in managing people and the high absentee rates due to sickness and stress. The offices and the rules by which they are administered are described as labyrinths and workers allege that there is a general ethos within them that says that money shall only be handed over to the young with the greatest reluctance.

For those young people who are of no fixed abode, DHSS offices are nightmares. Many workers believe that life is deliberately made difficult for these young people in order to deter them from squatting or sleeping rough. There are stories of the young being made to queue all day, then being told when they reach the top of the queue that the place is closing and to return the following day. Others are sent continually between local offices and the office at the Elephant and Castle that deals specifically with those of no fixed abode. There are consistent stories of the young being told, after days of this treatment, that their claims will not be processed for weeks. The young are admonished for being homeless and are told to return home as soon as possible. A wait of three to four weeks for a claim to be processed and money paid out is not unusual.

The experiences at local authority Housing Aid offices are similar. Young people are told consistently to leave London and return home as soon as possible. Those who live in the capital are advised that it will be years before they can be placed on any waiting lists. Local authorities, workers allege, see it as their duty to avoid paying out any money if they can possibly do so. Signing on has become an art in itself. Many young people are afraid to do so and are increasingly being alienated from the system. Proving identity is a nightmare. Some offices put people through a complicated process only to reject the identification that is offered, even though that identification may have taken some time to arrive. Other offices are more flexible and practical and will take written authorisation from project workers.

The problem with all this is twofold. The young are being incapacitated in dealing with bureaucracy as it is increasingly left to workers to take on the task as the only way of pressurising the DHSS to move. Second, many young people just do not want the hassle and are refusing to have anything to do with the whole process. This exacerbates their difficulties in finding a place in society and makes a life of begging, stealing or prostitution more attractive. The young person is kept continually at a disadvantage because he or she has no opportunity to learn how to use the system to the maximum benefit.

Further problems

There are other, less obvious difficulties, facing young people when they do finally receive money from the DHSS. There are the very real dangers of having it stolen because everyone knows what day money is handed out and which office young people have to claim from if they are of no fixed abode. The temptation to spend a large sum of money, usually back payment owed while a claim was being processed, can be quite great. Such a problem faced one young person who was sleeping rough. He complained in the course of a conversation that he had no money, nowhere to live and no idea where his next meal was coming from. In fact he looked well fed and healthy, a fact confirmed sometime after this comment when others in the group had become comfortable with the conversation. One made it very clear to the above individual that having spent a £160 back payment in two days, he deserved to be hungry and homeless.

The search for accommodation

Part of the rationale allegedly adopted by local authority councils in dealing with the demands of the young for housing is based on the fear that, if they make it easy for them, they will be encouraging them to leave home and so will be faced with an overwhelming demand for single accommodation. There is no doubt that such a policy seems to work. The young people in Central London projects and those who work with them despair at the lack of hope offered by housing departments.

It is contested that two-thirds of all twenty-year-olds live with their parents in Britain and at the age of twenty-three only a third of single young people will have left home (Howie *et al* 1985). Those who do leave are most likely to live in bedsits or hostels which contain some of the most serious sub-standard accommodation in the country (Waters 1982). This was underlined in a DHSS report in 1976 in relation to hostels. It complained that the facilities, regime and normal clientele of hostels made them unsuitable for young people. As a result, young people tended to look elsewhere for accommodation and in its absence squatted or slept out.

Not much has changed. John Patten, the then Housing Minister, reported in Parliament in January 1987 that a Department of Environment survey into the physical and social conditions of multiple-occupation housing in England and Wales found that they were among the worst of any sector of the housing market. They were often in poor physical condition, without adequate facilities, with minimum standards of hygiene, cleanliness and safety. High rents were often demanded for what were filthy and deteriorating properties (Rice 1987).

In London places for the young are declining. Eight hundred hostel places for the single homeless have disappeared over the past few years because of closures or improvements, and more and more young people have to live with the uncertainties of bed-and-breakfast accommodation, offering little space and even less privacy (Livingstone 1985). Tony Newton, the Health Minister, told Parliament in May 1987 that 24,900 young people between the ages of sixteen and twenty-five were in bed and breakfast in London between May and July 1985 (Locks 1985), while Ann Clarke, Camden's Director of Housing, said that of the 1,200 in bed and breakfast in that borough in April 1987, 25 per cent were single young people (Pyramid Project 1987).

For a few young people, the alternative to bed and breakfast is the offer of a place in a short-life property. There are many groups who offer this type of housing which usually consists of local authority stock awaiting demolition or modernisation. Some housing co-operatives and short-life users groups receive limited grants to do them up, but in effect such property offers conditions that vary little from squats. In 1984 over 4,000 local authority dwellings were on licence to short-life users in London. This implies that around 15,000 people were living in them, many of whom would be the young, single homeless (Livingstone 1985).

For the young person, bed-and-breakfast accommodation may often be a choice between sharing with a stranger or sleeping out on the streets. The number of hotels that offer bed and breakfast below £7 a night has dropped dramatically with the consequence that the young sometimes have to balance the need to eat with the need for shelter. Some choose to live out for a few nights and then go into bed and breakfast to build up their spirits and make use of the basic amenities. However, this choice has been restricted over the past year or so by the growth of families in bed and breakfast. Local authorities are block-booking places for families and the young single homeless are being pushed out because more money can be obtained from housing a family. Sharing a room with up to as many as three others is sometimes the only option for a young person and this causes frustration, insecurity and a great deal of resentment in the long run.

Up till April 1988, unless young people were part of an official resettlement programme, they had to move on after eight weeks in London. Hostels offering long-term accommodation are often full and are very difficult to get into and the jobs that are available do not offer enough money to enable a young person to gain any foothold in London's overpriced housing market.

Even when accommodation is obtained further difficulties arise. Some young people find hostels to be too impersonal, with rules and regulations that are inhibiting. Some workers are of the opinion that the old-style hostel, even with only twenty to thirty beds, is too large. The young prefer smaller units that allow for privacy yet also give companionship. For those in some form of rented accommodation, it is not uncommon to find landlords who are very difficult. Under the guise of being helpful they often treat young people in a way that is denying them their rights under the law and is often little short of outright harassment. Refusing to give rent books, taking Giro cheques before the young person can get hold of them, cashing them and handing back the cash that is left after the rent has been taken out, are common occurrences.

The experiences of those talked to in the London agencies underline the difficulties already outlined. Eight had slept the night previous to the discussion in a hostel or an emergency shelter of some sort. Five had slept rough, out in the open, and three had stayed in a squat. Four had found a place to stay on someone's floor, either in a bedsit or a bed and breakfast situation. None of those appeared to pay any rent. One had only just left home and had spent the previous night there.

Seven had slept some time in their declared 'home'. Six had been in the same place for a couple of weeks and the same number had spent a week, or less than a week, in the one spot. Only one had spent just one night in his declared place, that being on the roof of a block of flats from the early hours of a very sunny morning. He had spent part of the night at a club, part wandering the streets with a friend and part in an all-night cafe drinking coffee. In the fortnight immediately preceding the interviews most of the young people had slept in a combination of hostels, bed and breakfast, squats, friends' houses and out in the open. Only two had relatively 'settled' accommodation in that time, one at home and one in a friend's bedsit.

The obvious difficulties in finding somewhere to live were high on everyone's agenda. Without that security, everything else seemed less important. There were also criticisms expressed of existing provision. There was dislike not only for the physical accommodation but also for the rules and regulations that went with them. The young hated having to go out in the mornings at a set time and the fact that, once registered, they could not go out in the evenings. One had been so frightened and repulsed when he witnessed a sexual assault by one male on another, that he had left the accommodation to sleep in the open only a few hours after registering. Others felt the lack of somewhere to go in the mornings after sleeping out, to wash and change and go for a job interview, did not help their already slim chances of employment. Those who were in work and in hostel accommodation felt that hostel routines did not cater for the employed. Having to share a room often meant insufficient sleep before a day's work. Getting up was hard and not being able to secure their possessions when they left for work was a particular hardship.

The young single homeless are the lowest priority when it comes to housing. The housing they do receive so often assumes that they are incapable of coping with or unworthy of having better facilities. So often the young are left with large, impersonal hostels, poorly staffed, poorly run and poorly provisioned. And, what is of vital importance, they are still homeless, even in a hostel. So many places have move-on clauses that allow the young little time to catch their breath before going out again on to the circuit. As a consequence, getting a job and being able to give a hostel as an address is almost impossible.

The realities of homelessness
For some young people there is still a real ignorance of what being homeless in London really means, especially for those who come from outside the capital. Accommodation is clearly the major problem. It is difficult to cope or make sense of anything without a stable base, a security that can be called home. Accommodation is like gold dust, and even those homeless in London boroughs often have little idea about the extent of the accommodation shortage and the very slim chances they have of being considered for it.

Linked with this is the need to establish a ready source of income, to establish a claim with the DHSS, if unemployed, and to try to get a job that will give the individual a sense of purpose and a greater freedom to choose. However, the fact is that jobs are still very hard to find, especially jobs that pay an adequate wage that allows the young to pay for suitable accommodation. Social security regulations, especially the eight-week rule, make

it very difficult for young people and it is to their credit that many
can cope with the insecurity and panic that this engenders. There
is no doubt that this panic does overcome many others, those who
come to London completely ignorant of the realities. They are soon
deprived of possessions, money and what little hope they have
to start anew. For many, sleeping rough is the only option. It may
at first be an adventure but it soon becomes an experience that
few can cope with adequately.

The emotional price

The strain of being homeless and often at risk does take its toll.
Much of the depression and mental instability that young people
suffer begins here with the feeling of being trapped, not able to
return from where they have come, yet having nowhere else to go.

There is no doubt that agencies are becoming increasingly
worried about the steady growth of young people in their late
teens and early twenties who are suffering serious mental illness
and whose bizarre behaviour makes them more abandoned
among those who are already outcasts in our society. Their prevalence to violence, their psychotic and schizophrenic behaviour
make them unacceptable to the majority of existing agencies,
concerned as they are with the safety of their projects and those
who make use of them. It is said that such young people see
themselves as beyond help and workers have described aspects
of their lives that would not be out of place in some of the more
descriptive passages from the works of Dickens.

For others the strain is not so outwardly apparent, but the
consequences are just as dire. To this group belong those who
find accommodation but are unable to cope and to manage their
new-found independence successfully. Sometimes months, even
years, of being homeless can so erode living skills that some young
people find themselves back on the streets a short time after
reaching the longed-for goal, because of rent arrears and the
inability to survive on their own in a flat. Others are worn down
and defeated by the bureaucracy of living. With poor reading and
writing skills, they are unable to cope with the system.

Turning to prostitution

It is clear that there are many young people for whom the life of
a prostitute is seen to be the only way to survive. So many agencies
have expressed great concern at the growth of male prostitution

in particular and the dangers facing male teenagers. There is no doubt that this is a growth 'industry' in London, despite police efforts to curb it. The seriousness of the risks that young people face cannot be underestimated. Extreme physical and emotional violence, rape and death are part of the everyday gauntlet that the young person has to run, male or female. The threat of Aids has added a more sinister and serious dimension to their plight.

There has been less anxiety expressed about females and prostitution, though the very fact that it seems to be hidden far more in Central London since recent activities of the police in known areas, combined with the 'gentrification' of Soho, has not lessened the concern of agencies for young women. The dangers to them have not decreased and many feel that it is a herculean task for a young woman to move out of prostitution, not least because being young, female and homeless in London means being particularly vulnerable to exploitation and abuse.

Turning to crime

Some young people turn to a life of crime to survive. There is clear evidence from those who work with the homeless that homelessness does contribute to offending and re-offending. This 'revolving penal door syndrome' was outlined in a 1981 Home Office study (Andrews 1981). The young homeless quickly become prey to unemployment. Having no fixed abode they are often subject to signing-on difficulties and are prevented from finding a job. Often they have to wait weeks before a claim for benefit can be verified. In the meantime they often steal for food or cigarettes. Those who are caught are often more likely to receive a custodial sentence because they are of no fixed abode. When they are discharged they have accommodation and employment problems and the whole circular process starts again.

If evidence from Central London is to be believed, this pattern not only persists but has worsened. Begging or stealing from shops and selling the proceeds on the streets are common. During one interview one teenager pulled out from his pocket a pen, brand new and still in its cover, and asked for an offer to be made for it. Young people freely admit to living a lifestyle that is often on the edge of being illegal. Moreover, it is alleged by some workers that some young people are being encouraged to offend as the only way of getting into the system and receiving the support they need from statutory agencies.

Living with risk

As has been stressed, one of the realities of being homeless is that young people continually live for the moment, oblivious, perhaps intentionally, of the risks involved.

> Three young people, two boys and a girl, told of an encounter with a man who had bought them a meal and a couple of packs of lager the previous evening. He was a complete stranger to them who had stopped them in Oxford Street outside a Wimpy. The young people felt that the man had had ulterior motives for his generosity and the unanimous opinion was that they were probably sexual in nature. To their surprise he had left them at midnight thanking them for a good evening without any requests for favours. Such encounters may not be that rare, it is hard to tell, but the young people telling the story felt that it was worth any risks that may have been involved.

There was safety in numbers in that case and it can only be wondered whether any one individual would have taken up the offer on his or her own or fared as well. That offers are taken up despite the risks involved is freely admitted.

> One young lad told of an encounter with a man as he waited in the queue outside the Centrepoint night shelter. The man had offered him a meal and a bed for the night in a hotel. The lad had accepted, despite the danger and the obvious sexual requirements involved. He had felt that a good meal, a warm bed for the night and money in his pocket were well worth it. As he said, 'Anything is better than a night in Centrepoint'.

That is not so much a harsh and unfair judgement on the provision at Centrepoint, but more a comment on the priorities that some young people have when they are homeless and alone.

Limited support

As discussed in the next chapter, there is limited provision for all the young homeless and, for some of the groups mentioned above, their difficulties exclude them even from what is available. They share, in common with all the young homeless in London, the general scarcity of services that will allow them to talk at length and receive specialist counselling if they so wish. As one worker put it, the problem is that the young are given so much advice. They are passed from one agency to another without really having anything done for them. The young people stressed this lack of provision in their discussions. There is a feeling which they voiced, and which was echoed by some workers, that they are sometimes treated in a way that demeans and incapacitates them, so adding to the problem that some already have in motivating themselves.

When the young homeless do ask for help they find that there is very little that can be done for them in an emergency. So many agencies have stressed the lack of a provision that could provide a varied emergency-response service. As a consequence, it is felt by some workers that many young people self-select the problems they present to an agency. These are usually problems that the agency sees itself as dealing with and this guarantees entry to the young person. In the meantime, real needs are subsumed in the desire to find some sort of support for the here and now.

Conclusion

The short-term concerns of homeless young people are for accommodation, food, money and employment and for the coming day and its requirements. Most have the long-term aim to leave the circuit, find suitable permanent accommodation and to settle down—something that is common to every young person leaving home. The reality is that in London there is no way of knowing how long it will take to achieve those ideals. There is no doubt that many young people do survive the rigours of the homeless circuit, despite the odds, and go on to achieve that independence of thought and action for which they have strived for so long.

However, others do not survive and it is these young people that are an increasing cause of concern. For these young people advice as to what to do next is essential and agencies do offer that service. However, many need much more than just advice. They want time to talk about the sheer hell of trying to survive on the homeless circuit. They want the time, space and the expertise that is provided by a comprehensive counselling service and which is largely absent from the provision in London. Many workers are of the opinion that it is not enough just to put a roof over the heads of young people. They must also be taught the skills to survive, so that somewhere to live can really become a home, a safe and secure haven from where they can take their place in the community.

4   The support available

'Their calling, of binding up physical, mental and emotional
wounds, is a noble one. It requires seeing the child not as
what he has become through force of circumstances, but for
his own intrinsic worth, even if he is dirty, aggressive, rude,
ungrateful or "impossible"'. (Susanna Agnelli, *Street Children.
A Growing Urban Tragedy.*)

'Homelessness is every bit as socially isolating in this "Age
of Enterprise" as it was in all the other ages of enterprise
we have ever experienced. The task of offering love to the
unlovely is as hard now as ever it was.' (National Association
of Voluntary Hostels, *Annual Report 1987.*)

Statutory *v.* voluntary provision

Homelessness is a complex issue and there is no one particular
reason why so many young people get into difficulties because
of it. So much depends on the provision available, how one is
defined as qualifying for that provision, the reasons why particular
groups of young people have special problems, and the policies
and strategies that are put into motion.

Many would argue that homelessness is a political issue and
that it is the policies and strategies of government that are largely
responsible. Certainly the views of Beacock in 1979 that government reined in spending just as they were getting the message
that the key to the needs of the single homeless lay in appropriate
housing, would still be seen to be valid for the 1980s. Beacock notes
that the role of voluntary agencies has traditionally been to inno-
vate not to provide permanent facilities, yet such groups provide
most of the major provision for the young single homeless. While
this state of affairs continues, no long-term solution is possible,
for voluntary agencies do not have the wherewithal to effect
substantial reforms. The single homeless are clearly still a low
priority. Waters argues that the issues surrounding them—homelessness, criminality, disease and social disaffiliation—are very
much the responsibilities of housing, penal, health and welfare
departments. However, state policies are, in her view, 'institution-
ally based to cater for a vestigial group of dossers' (Waters 1982).

The role of statutory bodies

There is no doubt that these attitudes persist and often the responses of the statutory authorities are coloured by the assumption that the young homeless are dossers and inadequates on the one hand, and not really their problem, on the other. On the whole, voluntary agencies working with London's young homeless are very critical of what they argue is a less than helpful response to the problem by the statutory bodies.

Social services departments are, in general, taken to task for having little understanding of the needs of the young homeless. While allowances were made for the many difficulties suffered by the profession and recognition given to the fact that social workers are often badly overworked, there was a general concern among workers in the agencies that too many social workers had neither the training nor the common sense to cope. Individual social workers were criticised for being little different, on an emotional and developmental level, from those they had a duty to help. There is a general feeling that they are far too detached from the young homeless. The support they are able to offer is being rejected, because the young, deep down, often feel that social workers do not understand them or the nature of their difficulties and have little real concern for them as human beings.

Much of the same criticism is also aimed at the Probation Service. Some agencies admitted that their relationships with the service were awful. Largely this had to do with the way in which the service was seen to deal with those homeless young people who came into its sphere of influence. It is alleged that some probation officers encourage the young, not in so many words, to go out and offend as the only way in which they can receive the help they need.

One theory is that this is due to the way in which some probation officers have perceived themselves and their profession. They have ceased to see themselves as officers of the court and have begun to act in a manner more appropriate to the social and community work professions. This has affected the nature of the reports presented to the courts and, it is alleged, the recommendations for particular courses of action. The latter are a duty for probation officers as officers of the court, but it is alleged that they have often been absent or reluctantly given. Others have refused to comment on the provision recommended for the young person, regardless of its suitability to meet that young person's needs.

Consequently, it has been argued that judges have been more reluctant to put their faith in the service.

The feeling is that this trend has begun to be reversed and that officers are going back to more traditional roles. However, there is no doubt that there is a great deal of unhappiness in some agencies with the Probation Service. However, as in all cases, there are notable exceptions and other agencies cannot speak too highly of individual officers and the care given by the service to the young homeless.

To be fair to the statutory services the criticisms of them are a reflection of the policy responses to the young homeless in general. The fact is that no one statutory body sees itself as having a particular responsibility and the temptation for overworked individuals to pass that responsibility on is a hard one to resist. Until the young homeless are seen as a priority group with great needs, such criticisms are bound to exist.

The response of the voluntary agencies

The gap created by the reluctance of any statutory body to take responsibility for the young single homeless is filled to a certain degree by the voluntary sector. By their very nature, however, voluntary agencies are unable to offer the full and long-term support the situation demands.

Information and advice services

The service that is offered most frequently across the board to the young homeless in London is one of information and advice, usually on the consequences of being homeless, the risks involved, what accommodation is available, where and for how long, and the prospects for employment. This reflects the philosophy common to many of the agencies—to allow young people to make informed choices about the next steps they wish to take. Some of this advice and information is co-ordinated with other agencies, particularly when the young person is sent on to another agency as the next step. However, this co-ordination is not widespread across all agencies, but rather takes place between groups of agencies who, for reasons of philosophy or geography, are linked together.

One of the main criticisms voiced of the services that are offered stems from these narrow links. This argument says that by placing young people on the homeless circuit and sending them round it in circles until they drop out, the agencies are doing very little to meet individual needs, though they do guarantee their own individual existence. This argument goes on to criticise forums that exist to co-ordinate the continuation of such services, while giving little space to a debate about the issues involved, the nature of the young people being worked with, and the training needs of the projects' staff. This, it is argued, prevents the development of services and perpetuates the status quo.

This viewpoint is perhaps unnecessarily harsh, though it does reflect the concern by staff in some projects about the nature of the service offered and the direction in which it is going. Many agencies are clear that the young homeless would welcome a greater input from them and more opportunity to reflect. Some agencies do talk of giving counselling about issues wider than housing and employment. However, in the main, they are quick to point out that such counselling is informal, unstructured and inadequate. They are clear that, in general, workers feel unqualified to give such support and that time, space, lack of training and financial realities work against efforts to introduce it in a formal way.

Access to accommodation
A good number of agencies carry out what they see as successful resettlement programmes, helping the young person make the transition between moving out and away and finding a niche in the community that will be the basis for a settled future. Linked with this is the access a number of agencies have to permanent housing through a variety of London boroughs and housing associations, often direct from medium-stay provision that they themselves provide. Understandably, a great deal of time and effort is spent on providing this type of service, though the agencies lament that they are able to offer it to relatively few in number.

Even fewer offer a short-term provision, from a few days to a few weeks, to enable young people to catch their breath before moving on again. Feelings have been expressed that this type of service offers the young very little, though this is understandable. The need to keep such provisions available for newcomers, coupled with the lack of move-on accommodation and support, leaves projects with very little choice but to do the best they can in a short period. Very few have longer-term accommodation available and, where they do, they find that it is soon filled. The lack of accommodation in general for the young, and individual boroughs' interpretation of the 1977 Act with regard to their eligibility for housing in any particular area, means that short- and medium-term accommodation stays filled far beyond the time acceptable to the project and necessary for the young person to achieve full independence.

Other services

A few projects are able to offer crisis intervention for young people, though in the main they are geared towards specific groups, for example, those under sixteen, those in drugs or alcohol crisis, and young lads who are into prostitution. This is not a provision that is readily available and the costs involved, especially in staffing, make it difficult for small agencies to offer. Like much of the work in London, it suffers from the 'efficient versus effective' argument and is not seen to be justified on a twenty-four hour basis.

Likewise, outreach work suffers from the same economic constraints. It is not seen as cost effective and can be the first aspect of the work to suffer when staff shortages are present. The agencies largely rely on the young people coming to them. Very few are able to meet the young 'out there', as it were, and many argue that large numbers of young people are not being touched by existing services as a result.

A certain amount of provision is available during the day for young people. These offer sporting and educational activities. Some include outings, and most will try to help with finding accommodation or will link the young person with the relevant statutory service. Some also have washing facilities and one or two offer meals, clothing and furniture at a reasonable price. The problem facing this type of provision is that it is usually unavailable at the times when young people need it most—early mornings, evenings, weekends and bank holidays.

The recipients of service provision

Much of the provision is available for both males and females between the ages of sixteen and twenty-one. A number of projects raise that limit to twenty-five while others keep the twenty-one limit but are flexible according to individual need. Others see the age limits as operating only from the time of entry into the project and there are no automatic move-on requirements when the age limit is passed.

Very little is offered to those under sixteen, largely because of the legal difficulties involved. Most of that which is offered is offered by statutory agencies, with one or two notable exceptions. However, some projects are aware, if not absolutely certain, that some of the young people who use their services are under sixteen and most of them will try to put the young people in touch with the relevant statutory service. One or two agencies do take the risk of working with under-age youngsters, without informing the authorities, on the grounds that, unless they did so, these young people would stay clear of all supports because of their distrust and fear of adults. By gaining the confidence of these young people, these projects feel that they can eventually bring them back into the mainstream of support. However, it must be stressed that such approaches are the exception rather than the rule.

There are very few projects that offer services to one sex only. This is particularly difficult for females as mixed projects do tend

to be seen as male-dominated, though many accommodation projects do have specific male/female quotas to overcome that inbuilt discrimination. There are no projects specifically for gay males or for lesbians, though many would like to see such provision. Some projects, while open to all, will deal specifically with ethnic groups, especially the young Black and the young Irish. Other provision is available only to residents of particular boroughs, while some specific services are limited to clients of the West End Co-ordinated Voluntary Service for the Single Homeless (WECVS). Some of the drug projects are reluctant to refuse help to anyone, though, for practical reasons, residential projects have specific age and drug use criteria.

The limitations of service provision
Some projects make it clear that they will not turn away anyone who is in need. The only proviso put on that blanket acceptance is a refusal to allow anyone on the premises who, at the point of entry, is incapable of behaving in a manner that would not present a threat to others inside. Such people are sent away with an invitation to return once they have regained some control of themselves. Likewise, some projects promise not to reject anyone once they have been taken in. However, behaviour that is so disruptive that it causes serious harm to others is usually met by an expulsion. This may be limited to a twenty-four-hour ban, though in some cases it may result in permanent exclusion.

There are a variety of young people who, for a number of reasons, will not be helped by the projects. As has been stated, those under sixteen present serious legal difficulties to the vast majority of agencies, though the setting up of the Central London Teenage Project has gone some way to alleviate the needs of that group. However, as this project will readily admit, the law as it stands limits the scope of its work and hence the willingness of some young people to use it. The fight to set up a really safe house for the under-sixteen group is ongoing, and it is the feeling of many that until it is achieved some young people will risk living on the streets rather than face the possibility of their needs not being met.

The sixteen- to seventeen-year-old group also presents problems to the agencies. They can be quite a difficult group to manage, especially in residential accommodation. They often need twenty-four-hour support and their developmental stage sometimes means they are unacceptable to older teenagers who find them noisy, demanding and disruptive.

The statutory agencies may often be reluctant to do a great deal for such youngsters. The Probation Service has great difficulties in working with anyone under seventeen years of age and social services may also be reluctant to become involved because there is so little provision and because some agencies refuse to deal with particular young people. Such young people may have been through the system, seen it all, rejected all the available help, be unrealistic about their aims and be unable to state what they want out of life. These young people have so much inner pain that they live dangerously on the edge of life as a way of escape. There is a lack of any provision that will be willing to cope with these young people, not reject them in times of trouble, and be willing to take them back continuously, no matter what.

These young people are not even a substantial minority of the sixteen- to seventeen-year-olds. However, there are many young people whose lifestyles mean that agencies are often very reluctant to deal with them. Many make it clear that they cannot help those under the influence of drugs or alcohol, and residential projects are usually quite reluctant to help those who have had a history of drug, solvent or alcohol abuse. Those with a potential for violence or arson are likewise excluded, as often are those who are classed as troublemakers, who refuse consistently to accept the help that the project can offer and who seem to be bent on making difficulties for all concerned.

Most projects make it clear, both verbally and with written notices, that they welcome anyone from whatever racial or religious background and sexual orientation. Those young people who exhibit racial or sexist behaviour are excluded. In particular, projects are concerned with the needs of young gay men and young lesbians who find it especially difficult to cope. The workers feel that it is important to give this group every support, as many of them may well have suffered painful abuse in their home areas.

There are other groups of young people whom the projects are reluctant to help, even though they would like the opportunity to do so. Young pregnant women fall into this category. Projects are very limited in the scope they have to help these young women and most will direct them to statutory services, even though the latter may offer little more than bed and breakfast. Many workers lament the course of action they have to take, while feeling it is the responsibility of the statutory services to provide adequate support. The feeling is, however, that many young women fall through the system in bed and breakfast and never receive the help they are entitled to.

Young people who are the clear responsibility of the statutory services will also find that agencies are reluctant to give them any help. Many workers feel that, despite the lack of support a young person has received, and which may have led him or her to seek help in Central London in the first place, statutory services should be presented again with the young person's needs and badgered until help is given. How successful this approach is depends on the willingness of the agency and the young person to persevere. Likewise, those young people who are already being helped by another homeless agency in London will be encouraged to return for support so that lines of communication are kept open and the maximum help given.

Most projects find it impossible to help those young people who exhibit serious mental illness, because the nature of the support demanded is beyond the scope and abilities of staff. Likewise, physically handicapped young people cannot be looked after as the geography of many of the buildings, especially in Central London, actively works against them.

This is also a factor for some projects in their ability to offer continuous help to young people. Many buildings offer little space and even less privacy and certainly those projects who take young people directly off the streets are limited in the scope they can offer. Workers regret this but feel it is necessary if support systems are not to clog up. This is one factor in the maintenance of the 'circularity' of homelessness.

Groups that offer housing are often presented with making choices as to who is most in need. The most desperate are the priority, and those who are living rough or in insecure accommodation will be seen to first. However, there is a dilemma in this. Many young people come in looking for somewhere to live, even though they have a bed at home. The problem arises because that bed is often in a room that has to be shared with one or more members of the family and young people complain of feeling trapped and claustrophobic. Staff have to weigh up whether a young person can survive there in the short term, or whether conditions are so intolerable that a move out to join those living rough or in insecure accommodation is imminent. It is often not an easy decision to make.

The reason why agencies are reluctant to deal with particular groups of young people has largely to do with their scope and expertise. Most turn away young people because there is simply no provision in the project to deal adequately with them. As has been stated, this lack is sometimes physical and material. More often it is an admission that there is not enough staff to cope or that staff are insufficiently trained to handle either the particular young people or the difficult situations that may arise. This factor may be compounded by the presence of a number of volunteers in the project, or the fact that staff see their skills as dealing with one particular group of young people and feel that what they offer would be diminished by widening the scope of their work.

All these reasons can lie behind the admission that to accept particular groups of young people would undermine the project's work and threaten its safety. Others might argue that the need to present a safe, acceptable image to the project's sponsors, in order to guarantee funding, plays a more substantial role than agencies would like to admit.

The deficiencies in existing services
The agencies, themselves, make distinctions between the type of development that is needed in provision for the young homeless and the policies and situations that hamper them in their efforts to carry out existing work. The former has to do both with the gaps in existing services and the practical directions that might be followed to fill them. The latter is concerned more with the frustrations that agencies have to endure, given their size, their position in this work, and the general lack of priority it has in society in general.

Attitudes and motivation
The attitudes and motivation of the agencies have been questioned in the past. Brandon and his team talked of the appeal of the themes of marginality, loneliness, vulnerability and deprivation (Brandon *et al* 1980). Brandon likened the interaction to a fairy tale with the homeless being the victims, outsiders or sinners and the workers as champions, befrienders and saviours. Suspense and outrage come from the villains—property speculators, bureaucrats, drug pushers, dirty old men, pimps. He felt that therein lay all the drama of a *Babes in the Woods, Cinderella,* or *Little Red Riding Hood* and that it was no accident that *Cathy Come Home,*

Edna, the Inebriate Woman and *Johnny Go Home* have become the fairy tales of our time.

Brandon argued that the workers in the agencies were concerned, earnest and moralistic and found, perhaps, in the homeless their perfect complement. He felt that they had an investment in the growth of the problem and quantifying the homeless justified the viability of their projects. Even more importantly, the young homeless were needed as victims of a cruel and uncaring community.

These are harsh words and though today there are some who might uphold elements of that view, in the main there is nothing but praise for the work put in by the agencies, though some do question the lack of direction of individual projects. However, Brandon and his team tempered their thoughts with the explanation that in a metaphorical sense all of us may feel at times homeless, insecure, forsaken or disconnected. The affinity we feel with the young homeless may be based as much on those parts of ourselves that we repress as those we acknowledge.

Pressure on services

There is a feeling that some of the existing work is geared more towards the needs of agencies rather than those of young people. Work is often office-based with office-type hours, that is, Monday to Friday, largely carried out during the day and early evening. Little is available at the times when young people feel most vulnerable—evenings, weekends and national holidays. Linked to this is the dearth of support from specialist services out of hours, especially late evening and during the night.

All this is not so much a criticism, more a statement of economic realities. Such realities, however, do shape philosophical directions. One of the contentious issues surrounding the work in Central London is that it is more about doing things *for* young people as opposed to working *with* them. Young people do feel that they have to present themselves too often to projects as the projects want them to appear, not as they really are. The complaint is that very few projects are set up to relate directly to individual need, primarily because such work is too intensive of staff, time and, most of all, money.

It is not enough, the argument continues, to put a roof over someone's head. Too many young people are placed in bedsit accommodation at a time when they are, emotionally, not ready.

It is important for the young to achieve things for themselves. To do this they need time to look at what they say they need, to decide what they want, and to come to terms with what they will have to put up with until they can achieve these goals. They need to negotiate the right for space and time to think things over.

Much of the work that is done with the young is, of necessity, concerned with basics and gives them little space to catch their breath. The young rarely have enough time to learn to trust those who are offering help, so that they can help themselves and make decisions about their long-term futures and not just the immediate, important as that is. They need a great deal of supportive advice and counselling which has implications for projects about time, physical space and staffing. Eventually, it means finance, and the pressures on many projects just to survive often mean such developments cannot be taken up.

Certainly the greatest pressure on all those who work with these young people has to do with doing the best they can, with few resources, in as short a time as possible, so as not to cause hold-ups and blockages in the system. Without a plentiful supply of decent accommodation that can cater for a variety of needs and can be got into without extreme difficulty, much of the work for young people has to be about 'making do'.

The unsupported
The greatest gap is for sixteen- to seventeen-year-olds, many of whom want to make a new start. They need independent and affordable accommodation that consists of small units, offering support that can be opted into rather than forced upon them. Many agencies are reluctant to help this age group because of the sheer volume of need and the perceived difficulties of managing them. Overnight support plus intensive help is often a require-ment for this group. This costs a great deal of money because it demands staff with a great deal of expertise and coping skills. It does not stop there. This group needs to have accommodation that is both staged and developmental, with fail-safe procedures that do not mean instant expulsion because a young person falls down.

Older teenagers are badly in need of the same basic accommo-dation that will offer support if needed. Again the emphasis is on small, independent units that offer companionship and community but preserve privacy. Young people who are out at work sometimes find themselves at a disadvantage in hostel life which often caters more for those who are not in work. The daily procedures and the hostel structures reflect this. Likewise, for those young people out at college. All these groups need the privacy yet the support of small-unit housing.

Other young people have been highlighted as losing out in the present provision. Workers pick out those between the ages of twenty and twenty-five who, emotionally, are more like adolescents. They are not ready for a permanent, independent provision and have, in the meantime, to be in hostels with teenagers. This situation does not allow them the space to develop individually.

Pregnant women also fall into this latter category. There is little specialist provision that will cater both for their physical and emotional needs and which will give them security and support until they can move into permanent accommodation. As has been noted, the only option that is available for them, bed and breakfast, is a very detrimental one.

Specialist accommodation is also lacking for those young people for whom drugs are a major difficulty. At one end of the scale, agencies are reluctant to take in ex-drug users. There is a feeling that the drug user, like the alcoholic, is never free of drugs, and agencies feel that they just do not have the expertise to handle any breakdowns.

Others have highlighted the need to help those who opt to go on a de-tox programme. Many of these young people will be in unsuitable and unstable accommodation. All lack the support structures necessary to sustain their resolve while they wait the three to six weeks before a place on a programme becomes available. When they leave the programme, too many have to go back to the same, unsupported lifestyles, a factor that does not bode well for their staying off the habit. There is a dearth in London of different housing options that will be safe, supportive and not rejecting the instant the individual slips back into the drug habit. Support that is tolerant and which can help with housing, education and employment is essential. It is a costly and a difficult provision and those factors largely contribute to its absence in Central London.

There is also little or no provision for those young people who exhibit bizarre behaviour, who may be psychotic, schizophrenic or have problems of severe personality disorder. This group, a cause of growing concern, may include some who might have been in hospital and have moved out under the care-in-the-community programme. There is a strong feeling that this group has been badly neglected by the health services and has been left to its own devices. There are other young people in this group who have not had specialist help yet badly need it. They require a place of safety while they wait for provision to be found that can best help them.

Then there are those adolescents who are simply going through a rather difficult phase of their development. Their needs are too great to be coped with in existing provision because they are so vulnerable and fearful. Accommodation that can offer security, and specialist counselling that they can accept, are rarely available.

Little co-ordination and research

There is another element lacking in present provision that is not widely recognised, but is apparent to those who might be said to be a little apart from the task of offering a day-to-day service. There is some emphasis on co-ordination of work in Central London among those who belong to WECVS with some support and training for those working with the young homeless. In general, though, this work is characterised by a lack of co-ordinated support, a wide ignorance of what others are doing in the same field of work and a dearth of specialised training for staff. There are some attempts to co-ordinate policies and approaches, but the general picture is one of fragmentation. There are strongly held opinions that the co-ordination that does exist may have more to do with smoothing over the cracks in approaches and philosophies, than debating the issues about working with the young homeless, identifying their needs and formulating a united response.

Linked to this issue is the general absence of any detailed research into the whole aspect of youth homelessness together with the lack of understanding of individual need. There are notable exceptions to this, but in general projects lack the systems and expertise that would enable them both to record and reflect on the work they do and to translate that into provision to meet future need.

Existing provision is very much a cluster of work that lacks a core that would offer real co-ordination and bring all the projects together as a group of interdependent, yet independent pieces of work, offering a highly skilled, multi-disciplinary approach.

Such a core would enable real communication between all groups and not just among some of the clusters, as at present.

Conclusion

That some young people refuse to use existing services is, in part, a reflection of the nature of those services. There is an argument that says that there is a naivety present that often ignores what is important for young people and which places the pursuit of a particular ideology before what is practical and necessary in the short term. This does make it hard for agencies to work together in a co-ordinated fashion, because individual philosophical perspectives cannot easily be married. However, there is no suggestion that this is an insurmountable problem and one of the characteristics of this work is the high level of individual commitment to the young people shown by agency staff.

Nonetheless, the young homeless are suffering because of this and are being forced on to a circuit that is demeaning to them as human beings. As a result, many feel that the young are voting with their feet and the fear is that unless efforts are made to change direction by all concerned, there will be a continual emergence of a substantial sub-group who have little faith in society and much less regard for that which society holds dear. Many workers have expressed this anxiety and argue that beginnings must be made by bringing in more workers who understand the scene, can accept the young people as they are and where they are at emotionally, and be prepared to work effectively with them. The commitment is there, but there is a lack of training and direction.

In outlining the deficiencies in existing provision, there is no attempt to offer criticisms of individual agencies who work hard within tight economic and strategic limitations. There are many factors that work against the provision of effective services in London. The lack of any co-ordinated local or national guidelines to deal with the problems presented by the young homeless is the major factor. The demise of the GLC has left a vacuum, and there is no one organisation with the overview and foresight that could bring people together. There is no doubt that those in the field feel that such an organisation is necessary. They would welcome any approach that could effectively give both coherence and a direction to work for the young single homeless in London and, at the same time, open new doors towards a greater understanding among those who have the power to effect change in their lives.

Part two

5 The Afro-Caribbean dimension

'How can I, a white man, become Black? To be Black means that your heart, your soul, your mind and your body are where the dispossessed are.' (Dr James H Cone, *Black Theology, Black Power.*)

'There are more than enough statements, resolutions and publications on racism—they all condemn it and call for programmes to eradicate this plague of modern humanity. What is now urgently needed are actions, vigorous and far-reaching actions.' (J Vincent, *The Race Race.*)

The young Black homeless

It goes without saying that the difficulties that the young homeless have apply across the board to all backgrounds and ethnic origins. However, it is also true to say that for a whole variety of reasons the difficulties facing young Black people who are homeless are very particular to that group, and, because of their position in society, are probably much greater in terms of intensity and effect.

The size of the problem

Very little information is available on the level of homelessness amongst young Black people. In general, the young Black homeless are underrepresented in Central London agencies, though most agencies would feel they see between 20 and 35 per cent of those who use the project as belonging to an ethnic minority group.

Black homelessness in London is very much a London-based problem. In a report carried out by Angela Yapp (1987), under the auspices of the Piccadilly Advice Centre whose experiences of young homeless Black people in Central London were looked at, 80 per cent of Black respondents came from London as opposed to 35 per cent of Whites. Of the 35 per cent of young men who had slept rough for one night, 71 per cent were Black. However, there is some evidence of growing applications for accommodation from young people who have come into London to take up places

at educational institutions or to start jobs and who have no friends
or relatives to contact.

It is the feeling among young Black people, as reported by those
who work with them, that the Central London agencies are very
much White, middle-class services that do not meet their needs
and there is some fear, real or imaginary, of being treated unfairly.
Young Black people who are homeless are likely to find accommodation initially with relatives and friends and only look for advice
when the situation of moving from friend to friend and staying
for a few days at a time becomes intolerable.

It is at this point that projects like *Ujima* will be approached.
Ujima receives requests for housing from around 250 to 300 people
a month. At best it can accommodate 30 of these. In 1985/86 it
had 3,527 people on its waiting list: 1,516 males and 2,011 females.
One hundred and fifty-three were between sixteen and seventeen
years of age with 2,121 between eighteen and twenty-four years
of age. The racial mix was as follows:

	%
West-Indian origin, born in UK	50.9
West-Indian origin, born in the West Indies	14.6
African origin, born in UK	0.4
African origin, born in Africa	15.2
Asian origin, born in UK	0.9
Asian origin, born in Asia	1.4
European origin	3.6
Others	13.0

It is generally accepted that while young Black people are under-
represented in Central London, they are by far overrepresented
in the total young homeless population. Threshold's study in
Wandsworth emphasises just that and is probably quite typical.
Forty-one per cent of their applicants were of Afro-Caribbean
origin, 5 per cent Asian, 6 per cent African and 6 per cent Irish.

The nature of Black homelessness
Much of Black homelessness will remain hidden and this has to
do with the nature of the Black homelessness circuit. Most young
Black people will still have relatively close family links and many
families will still be quite shocked if a relative, even a distant one,
turns up on their doorstep looking for a place to stay. Most will

take the young person in and find help for him or her. The reasons for this are cultural and historical. Many older West Indians have suffered from a lack of accommodation, especially on entry into Britain, and can empathise with the difficulties the young are facing. Likewise, the young homeless are likely to find a welcome on friends' floors which they often prefer to that which a homeless agency can offer. Many, too, will live in squats while waiting to take up some form of accommodation that has been promised.

The pull of English culture vis-à-vis traditional West-Indian culture has an impact on the leaving home process. Emigration to England has meant, in many cases, the loss of the traditional extended West-Indian family. In England the emphasis is so often on the nuclear model with the expectation that young people, at the age of eighteen, ought to go off and find their own place to live. Friction arises when the Black youngster comes up against what is often a very strict, Victorian-type response in a society where the White counterpart often has a great deal more freedom from seemingly more 'liberal' parents. The young Black person does not feel good in this situation and is unable to relate to his or her parents. The desire to leave home immediately and assert his or her own independence is overwhelming.

Many young Black people are forced to leave home simply because there is too little space in what are often large and growing families. Often these families live in poor accommodation that does not have the bed or living areas to accommodate everyone. Older children are encouraged to move out in their late teens so that the rest of the family can have more breathing space.

Some homeless young people end up on the streets at a loose end. The temptation for many, no matter from what racial group, to commit petty crime is very strong and many workers feel that there is quite a group of these homeless and rootless young people who have offended in this way and have been caught. Because of racist attitudes in society, young Black people are more likely to be picked up and the shame for families of having a son or daughter in prison is too hard to bear, especially for those with fairly stark and rigid attitudes to life. They reject the young person who may sometimes be attracted to what some workers have called a 'lifestyle of black crime'. Likewise, a young woman who becomes pregnant may well initially face rejection from home, particularly from strict and rigid religious Afro-Caribbean parents, anxious to avoid what they see as a scandal in their local community. In many cases, time is a great healer and parents do accept the situation, without always necessarily having the daughter back home to live.

The parents of some young people return to their roots in the Caribbean and many others go to America to better their lot, leaving their children behind to be brought up by relatives. These young people find it hard to settle and are sometimes attracted to a life of crime. The parents of others send their children to this country to be brought up and educated here with relatives. For whatever reason, they have never left their homes in the Caribbean and this has left their children alone and insecure. Despite the care of relatives, many of these young people are only too anxious to leave home and set up on their own.

Part of the cultural heritage of young Black people has instilled a sense of self-reliance, so when they leave home, in whatever circumstances, they have a great desire to make good for themselves. In this way they mirror what has happened to their own parents when they moved from the Caribbean to this country and this has become part of their culture, part of their thinking. They intend to make good without seeking the help of other people and will only accept it when circumstances dictate they have to take it, especially if it involves the statutory services.

Workers emphasise that most young Black people have learned to 'hustle' and stand on their own two feet. They have learned to do this, moreover, without attracting attention, particularly that of the police. As a result they have adapted quickly to sleeping rough, or in a friend's house, or in a squat and have managed to slip away quickly and quietly before attracting attention. They have learned to acquaint themselves very quickly with situations and to keep away from anything that might place them in the limelight. In addition, workers feel that the sub-groups of the Black homeless are very protective to each other and because of the pressures and difficulties they face as Black people, they are perhaps much closer to each other than their White peers may be in similar circumstances.

Living with racism
Certainly, the main pressure that the young Black homeless faces has its roots in the institutionalisation of racism in society. There

is no doubt that West-End agencies have worked and are continuing to work at the elimination of racist attitudes and practices, both in their own structures and among the young people with whom they work. However, they admit that their services are often seen by Black people as White and middle class, whose values have little in common with those of the young Black homeless. This is not so much intentional but more a consequence of the difficulties of life in general, the generation gap between worker and young person and the class structures in British society. This, according to Black workers, makes for a big divide between White and Black.

There is no doubt that the experiences of many young Black people with 'White' authority have left them feeling very uncomfortable to say the least, so when they become homeless in London they fight shy of an authority that in the past may have left them feeling inadequate and second class. They take it for granted that 'White' authority will treat them unfairly and they prefer to sleep rough or live in very difficult conditions rather than risk the help that White organisations can offer. Some are now accepting such help through the support of Black housing groups. These groups will recommend a place to a young Black person and give him or her support in it where they judge that the White organisation has made a determined effort to have a proper ethnic and sexual mix in the accommodation proposed.

Workers point out that racism, although it affects the young homeless now, has its roots in the past and the history of the families of these young people. Many of their parents came to this country and were forced to do work that required them being away from the parental home for the most important part of a child's day, in the morning when he or she got up and in the evening when school was finished. The consequence was a generation of latch-key children forced to spend so much of their time alone, lacking the care and control of their parents.

The accommodation these parents had to accept when arriving in this country from the Caribbean was often of poor quality and too small for their needs. It is hard for these parents and their children not to feel that the aim of government was, and still is, to keep them down and prevent them bettering themselves.

Thirdly, when the Afro-Caribbeans arrived in Britain, their White neighbours knew nothing about them. Their knowledge of Black people was limited to what they saw in the cinema and this tended to be patronising. It did not differentiate between races and cultures, but lumped people together on the basis of skin colour.

This ignorance on the part of the indigenous population soured relationships with the immigrant community and led to misunderstanding, resentment and violence. Many Black people felt they were continually being brought into conflict with their White neighbours and this led to divisions and separations to keep the peace. This is the basis of present divisions and hostility and workers feel that little was done by government then, and little is being done now, to educate White people into an understanding of the Afro-Caribbean way of life.

The pattern of life forced on the Black immigrant undermined family life and deprived his or her children of basic and necessary parental care. As a result many of the present generation have grown up without that essential stability in family life. The neglect they have experienced has led to a growing sense of alienation from their parents and has, as a result, made communication difficult. Other children, having initially been left at home in the West Indies while their parents struggled to find a niche in British society, felt that their parents were strangers to them when they were eventually brought over. This alienation and emotional loss has no doubt had a detrimental effect on the development of many Afro-Caribbean young people and many workers would argue that it is the reason for the levels of disturbance among the present generation. Certainly, the West-End agencies have noted this trend with growing concern.

Another aspect of this has had to do with the way in which Black people were treated in the past when they wanted to express their feelings. Many of this earlier generation were labelled mad and unstable because Black people are less conservative in their expressions of frustration and anger than their White counterparts. Rather than hit someone or destroy property when they were hurt and insulted, they would prefer to scream and shout. This was not acceptable in White society and often a Black person would be taken to court for disturbing the peace. There questions would be asked about mental stability and a history of mental illness. This would insult and inflame the Black person who would often, understandably, react at such accusations, so emphasising to the White judiciary the very 'madness' that had been in question.

The effects on the children of such parents accused of being mad or bad, or both, were quite profound. Instilled in their conscious-ness was the impression that White society saw them as people to be patronised and labelled as an inferior 'species'. There is no doubt that such individual and institutional racism still exists, preventing the young from taking their place in society. The slow pace at which this racism is being dismantled does not give young people enough optimism to feel that theirs will be the generation that will be finally accepted as people of worth and be allowed to play a full part in British society.

Those working with the young Black homeless feel strongly that unless people are aware of and understand this background, they will not begin to have a clear conception of Black homelessness in London today. In addition, one could not begin to comprehend the difficulties of the task facing young Black homeless people as they strive to make sense of their parents' culture and history on the one hand and the nature of British society on the other. The conflict between their ideals and aspirations and those of their parents has its roots in history and resources made available to help them must take account of that history.

Accommodation difficulties
There is an increasing number of young Black people who have gone through various stages of homelessness before coming in to seek help. They are first homeless from home. They often go then to relatives who help them for a while, before they feel the need to move on again. Often they will move to friends' houses and remain there for a considerable period. Eventually, they drift from one friend to another on a night-to-night basis and then come into agencies to ask for somewhere permanent. Another group, noted by Ujima, are those who are new to London. In common with all the homeless, they have a great deal of difficulty, not only in finding somewhere to live, but also being accepted on a local authority housing list because of qualification requirements.

It is said that many young Black people prefer to live rough or with friends rather than stay in hostels or bed and breakfast. There are a number of reasons for this. Partly it has to do with the fact that many of these places are run by White people and the feelings young Black people will have about being misused. Partly, it is the cramped facilities of many of these places that make young people feel that they are concerned with making money primarily and not with giving a quality service to their clients. Partly too, their friends' floors are often in better condition than the alternative accommodation and it is culturally difficult for them to sleep on beds or use linen that have been first used by others. This is sometimes true of short-life property as well and that, coupled with the fact that it can take a long time just to be placed on a waiting list for such property, makes the young reluctant to be part of such a scheme. Most want their own place, empty, where they can start from scratch and build up their own furniture and equipment. The problem with this approach is that it makes it difficult for them to be placed on the local council lists, whereas accepting short-life places can mean being passed on fairly quickly.

Many young people feel trapped in their local boroughs. They are either unemployed or in low-paid jobs, so they lack the financial ability to move out, and local authority regulations about eligibility for housing mean they are unable to move elsewhere. Even those who are given a place in a short-life housing property often find themselves staying three to four years instead of six months to a year, which is preferable, because of the lack of move-on property. When such property becomes available, young people are often reluctant to move, because after three or four years they are settled and have friends and contacts in that area. More permanent property may be situated at the other end of the borough and young people can be quite reluctant to move on and start again.

Unemployment

Unemployment is probably one of the major reasons why young Black people leave home. Certainly workers feel that the drift of young Black people from cities outside of London into the capital is due to the high level of unemployment in many ethnic areas. Even when they do get jobs, they are often of the low-paid variety which makes it difficult for them to cope and impossible to find accommodation.

Some parents can place very high expectations on their children. They expect them to find a job, despite the problems surrounding employment for young Black people, and often despite the fact that one or both parents may be unable to find work themselves. Part of this has to do with how the Afro-Caribbean sees the value of work. You are not seen to be fully a man or a woman unless you are able to work. So many young people are quite depressed and disillusioned at their employment prospects and many are fast losing the will to find work or continually to accept the racial harassment that is too often part and parcel of the workplace.

Young Black people feel strangled in a system that says a person has to work and makes it so that only those in work are rewarded. Yet this same system prevents Black people from working, something that is reflected in the high proportion of Black people among the unemployed as opposed to their proportion in the community as a whole. The young unemployed are learning to survive by forming sub-groups with other young Black unemployed and helping each other to cope.

This phenomenon can be seen particularly in relation to the

DHSS. In common with their White counterparts, young Black people have experienced frustration, anxiety, sarcasm and open hostility in local offices. Black workers feel strongly that the lack of training among DHSS staff, the shortages in the numbers of staff available at any one time to deal with difficulties and the general lack of sensitivity and good manners in dealing with the young unemployed, contribute largely to making the offices places of turbulence and violence. The young are tired, frustrated and hungry and are responding to this violence with violence. They are learning that the only way to get something in this life is to be loud and aggressive and to turn the fear that the system engenders back on to those who perpetrate it—the authority in the offices.

As a result there has been a great upsurge of emotional violence in DHSS offices. The young receive this violence and give it back with interest. They cope by refusing to keep appointments, or by shouting and demanding every penny that is their due when they do attend. They often pool together in groups of four or five and challenge the fear and lack of dignity shown to them by the authorities. Sometimes they break the law in order to get what they want. They are attracted by the television images of the good life and want this for themselves now and are not willing to wait for it any longer.

Care systems

One of the anxieties expressed by all workers was the worry about the way in which young Black people out of care and adrift were trying to cope. There is a consensus that all homeless young people out of care, Black and White, are the most difficult group to cope with. Some groups limit the numbers of these young people that they will take simply because they are hard to handle and need a level of supervision and support that is very demanding on existing resources.

Some of those in care end up in prison for short spells and are left adrift and at risk when they are let out. For the younger group, especially the sixteen- to seventeen-year-olds, help that could be offered by the Probation Service is sometimes not as forthcoming as it might be. Probation won't take on anyone under seventeen and there is a particular gap in provision for those who are Black, male or female. This is a problem, some feel, for the referrers and not the institutions who are crying out for Black referrals. It is alleged that some probation officers have the idea that young Black people will not conform to the rules and regimes of a hostel. Yet hostel managers argue that they are no more difficult a group than their White counterparts and in many cases do so much better. It is felt that some probation officers assume the young Black person will reject a hostel and they never give them the opportunity to state their own opinions on the issue.

A third concern is for young Black people who are placed in care in homes outside of London away from their communities and contacts. This group finds it very difficult when they have to return and have problems in relating back to their Black society. There is no doubt that workers are very concerned at the lack of care shown to those who are the responsibilities of local authorities. Not only are such young people ill-prepared to leave the care system and set up for themselves, but they are also not given the level of support they need. There is dissatisfaction with a social services system that is seen to be under-resourced and inefficient and, in terms of young Black people, staffed by too many White social workers, straight out of college, with little idea about how young Black people have lived and scant understanding of their real needs. There is no doubt that many are very anxious about this situation and are urging that steps be taken to remedy it.

Difficulties facing Black communities
Those working with the young Black homeless have an additional burden to that carried by White groups. The context of their struggle to alleviate the difficulties of the young in their communities has to do with the way in which the immigrants came to this country and their difficulties receiving recognition.

Some of those who came to Britain from the Caribbean in the 1950s did so to earn enough money in about five years to be able to return home and help improve their own country. That never happened for so many, and, like the Irish of the same generation, they were caught between not being able to return, yet not wanting to stay. Some had borrowed money to make the trip, money that could never be repaid. Britain became a trap which they could not escape from. As a new generation was born and brought up, attitudes changed. Black people are now part of British life and will be part of it for generations to come.

Yet many difficulties remain before, like their American counterparts in the 1960s, they can achieve recognition and acceptance.

The context of their difficulties lies in how authority views them as Black people and how younger generations are taught to understand them as a people with a history and a culture that have been indivisibly linked with Britain down the centuries.

The immigrants of the 1950s saw great opportunities which they felt at that time were not present in the Caribbean. So many have been disappointed by what they have received. Workers talk of the feelings they have that Britain's educational system is not adequate for the needs of its Black youngsters. They say it pays no attention to the feelings and thoughts of young Black people. It is afraid to get close to them, to touch them, to try and understand where young Black people are coming from. This places additional burdens on many families who struggle to come to terms with their youngsters caught between two cultures. Some of these families may have been set up more on the basis of economics than love and the tensions within them have led to many a youngster being pushed out.

In the Caribbean these youngsters would have been taken in by the wider family and cared for. However, in common with many families of all cultures in British society, this wider family support is not present. Slavery initially destroyed many family systems in the Caribbean. Just as these systems were being restored they had to be uprooted again; this time by the need to seek work in another country for the good of the community and the future prosperity of the land. Emigration destroyed many close family networks and in Britain there are often no elders in the community to go to for support and wisdom, because that type of community no longer exists. Black people feel they have lost their culture and have a sense of alienation and not belonging in Britain.

This alienation has had a profound impact on young Black people who are experiencing many emotional difficulties with parents. There is a feeling that, with support, some youngsters can survive at home and be helped to make sense of the differences they have with adults. However, many others do not fall into this category and can sometimes be very difficult to deal with. Some agencies speak of about 30 per cent of those they come in contact with suffering from what they term 'a severe emotional handicap', 'extrovert people' who are not taken account of in an 'introvert society'. A wide range of educational provision is necessary to help such youngsters cope, in addition to books and newspapers that are particularly related to young Black people, their history, their culture and the way they lead their lives. Much more needs to be done to help their White counterparts in school to understand that history and culture. For those dealing with homeless Black youngsters the problem is that they can only try to cope with the symptoms of distress. It is outside of their scope to remedy the problem.

Part of the remedy lies in the way in which statutory services offer support. Accommodation that is not supported by training, education and emotional help is not enough. Some young Black people, workers feel, have a crisis of identification, between 'acting' Black and 'thinking' Black. Some statutory provision is criticised for enforcing a Black lifestyle, yet ignoring Black culture. White agencies overcompensate in their attempts to identify with Black lifestyles. This can often be a negative process in that it can be more an attempt to mould young Black people into a pattern of life that does not take into account what they truly want to be.

The stereotype of a young Black person sleeping all day and partying all night has nothing to do with being Black, but more to do with being young, unemployed, often homeless and without hope. In that context such a lifestyle is common to all ethnic groups, but when it is referred only to young Black people it can lead to racial stereotypes of Black and bad. Young Black people are often neither asked what they need nor listened to when they say what they want. They are often placed in youth custody on the pretext that they won't accept probation hostel routines. It is no wonder, as agencies stress, that the Afro-Caribbean community has the largest proportion of those in mental hospitals, in prison and of those who are homeless. Yet those who work with young Black people argue strongly that as young people they are little different behaviour-wise to their White counterparts and are often more reliable and well behaved in projects.

As long as society in general, however, has these attitudes, the plight of the young Black homeless will remain. The ability of the Black community to cope with its homeless young people cannot be sustained indefinitely without support from the wider community. Many workers of all groups feel that our society has lost its sense of identity, has become too Americanised and has replaced old values with a belief in the material, beliefs that are being passed on to the youth of today.

The end of World War Two promised a united community that would fight against oppression and injustice. That has not happened and some Black people feel that that war is being continued in our communities' streets, except now we are fighting each other. Black people are fighting for a piece of the community cake, yet they feel that all they can fight for are the crumbs left over after White people have taken what they want. They feel that if the country goes short, it is the Black person who feels the pinch.

Black workers feel that there is a great lack of understanding in the White community about Black needs. Much of this lack of understanding is added to by the way in which the media report Black people and the way in which they are made out to be extremist and bad. The truth is distorted and people despair at the opportunity of being able to tell it as it is, no matter how unpalatable that is to society in general.

The responses of society and government
Society, workers feel, responds by trying to keep the Black person down, as it has done in the past, though now the methods used are more sophisticated. As soon as they try to live within the rules, the rules are changed. Black people often feel they have no place in society. The police are people to be afraid of, not a body to support and defend them. The problem of Britain today, as Black people see it, is that it has a society that stresses only the individual's need, without seeing that need within the context of the community as a whole. As long as the whole is ignored for the sake of the individual, Black people will never be allowed to have a place in society. In that context it is hard for Black people to join the police and defend a society which they have no part of and material possessions which they can never share. Yet unless society learns to share its wealth with all, it will be doomed. Society has to get itself together and teach its members to live as human beings. Technology should be used to that end, not to exploit and enslave one's neighbour. Without this willingness to fight for our values as people, we can never co-exist as different racial groups.

Government has a unique role to play here. Racism is ultimately a commercial tool and a means of keeping power. Change will only come when government thinking is so altered that the laws and conditions that keep racism at work are swept away. The first aspect of that change is an admission that racism is bad and has to be eradicated from all levels in society. This is the major hurdle to be attacked and unless it is, it will be futile to talk about resolving Black homelessness, for so much of that homelessness is rooted in racist attitudes.

Black people feel they have little voice in national or local government and so in the means of bringing about change. They sometimes feel that local government sees them only as threats, not as human beings. Thus they are forced to work in what some workers have termed 'a twilight society', within a system that is sparing with the help it gives to Black people, never giving projects the amount of money they need to be effective. Social services are criticised for being less interested in the Black person as a human being and more in the strengths and weaknesses of the project. Yet they have no grasp of the fundamentals projects are trying to deal with and no understanding of the homeless Black youngster and the difficulties he or she faces.

Black workers feel that no one wants to give them the benefit of the doubt. No one trusts them with the means to help their communities, despite the plentiful supply of money that is around. Part of this mistrust is the view that Black people make poor managers and administrators. Yet nothing has been done to help a society whose roots were in being a labour force that was, unlike its Indian counterparts, never allowed to manage its own affairs. There is consequently little respect for Black workers who have been brought up in this society, who have lived through the changes that have taken place and who are able to get young Black people involved. Only these people could help to begin the process of putting things right between Black and White. White people have neither the knowledge, understanding, nor trust of young Black people to make things work.

There is a skill in dealing with young people who are confused and alienated and only when White people respect Black managerial abilities can that change be effected. Black people have to speak out and deal with the Black predicament. White people cannot put themselves in a Black person's place and speak with a singularity of purpose. Their purpose will, of its nature, always be mixed. It is not possible to have Black spokesmen in a White context. This is why Black agencies argue that Black workers be given the opportunity to work with young Black people, even if the workers do not necessarily have the formal training. They have skills that no training course can give, skills that arose out of their own experiences as Black people in this society. There is a strong request to authorities to invest seriously in such skills, if they wish to make an impact among the young Black homeless.

This is the context of Black homelessness. One has to accept that in dealing with the young Black who is homeless, on the margins and disillusioned, one is also dealing with the disillusionment of the parents of such young people, parents who came to this country with so many promises and who now find themselves trapped in a land that does not seem to care for them.

6   The Irish dimension

'The young arrive from Ireland, are unable to find employment and drift into substandard housing, or a squat, or sleep rough. Some fall victim to drug abuse or flirt with alcohol escapism and far too often fall victim to male and female prostitution . . . Racist stereotyping of Irish people as stupid and violent is considered to be a factor in the lack of self-esteem, helplessness and depression perceived in single homeless Irish people.' (CARA, The Irish Homeless and Rootless Project, *A Profile.*)

The young Irish homeless

The young Irish homeless are also affected by being immigrants and they too have needs that centre around their position in society and an understanding of their history and culture. There are many Irish centres in London, but they exist for a settled group from a previous migration and are related to an Ireland of long ago, rather than the needs and demands of the 1980s.

Due to social and economic conditions, the young are leaving Ireland in great numbers and agencies feel that the scale of emigration is reaching unprecedented proportions. The Irish Centre reported a 14 per cent increase in 1986 and felt that that was surpassed in 1987. Around 75 per cent of these were under 25 years of age, a reminder that Ireland has the youngest population in Europe, with half its population falling into this age group. There has been, however, little corresponding increase in the resources necessary for them.

Ireland has a long history of emigration among its people, especially to Britain, so much so that it is almost unnoticed. Of all immigrants, they have a high profile in national life. Thus it is surprising that some feel that they are not understood as a group, that their young people feel insecure and threatened and very much second class. Indeed some workers argue that the Irish are very much an ethnic minority, suffering all the indignities and discrimination of other ethnic groups. Yet, because they are White, they are not immediately seen to have a problem. Young Irish people complain of a lack of understanding of them and their culture among the agencies in London. Some speak of being ignored or being made fun of because of their accents and the way they express themselves.

Many are leaving Ireland because of difficulties with their parents and the lack of opportunity, especially in employment. Many are making it clear that they cannot live in Ireland any more and have no intention of returning. There is a strong dislike of the influence of the Catholic Church in government and in society in general, and many are wary of using Irish agencies in London because of the presence of priests and nuns in management and social work capacities.

For some, this dislike has to do with the nature of the difficulty that has led them to leave Ireland and which, they feel, would receive little sympathy from the Catholic Church and its representatives, because of the stance taken on some moral issues. Some young women who are unmarried and pregnant or wish to have an abortion come into that category, as do young lesbians and gay men whose sexual orientation would be an anathema to many of their countrymen and women. For such young people it would be impossible to survive in the small towns and villages where they have been brought up. The somewhat claustrophobic atmosphere and lack of individual privacy in community life would leave them no option but to move away.

Problems facing the young Irish

The main aims of young Irish people are to find work and accommodation and to settle quickly in Britain. Many will have been without work for some time and may have used the last of their dole money to fund the journey over.

Others, leaving school at fifteen, come penniless and look to claim from the DHSS here. It is at this point that so many run into difficulties. In Ireland, dole and supplementary benefit offices are in the same place. Here they are not, and the young are easily confused by a system they are not used to and often lack the advice to make adequate claims. Secondly, there is the problem of adequate identification. Many have only a baptismal certificate which is not accepted for social security purposes. It usually takes some time for birth certificates or passports to be sent over and in the meantime many young people are destitute and stuck here without any means of making money.

Discrimination in DHSS offices is a common complaint. The young are subject to a fair amount of abuse and hassle because they are Irish. The main accusation against them is their Irish nationality. It is argued that because they have put no money into this country, they do not deserve to receive benefit and some have been told bluntly to leave and return to Ireland.

Discrimination is also practised in employment. Some young people have been refused work because they are Irish and agencies feel that the situation of previous decades, where 'No Irish Need Apply' notices were put up, has returned, though in a more subtle form to avoid accusations under the Race Relations Act. Even when young people do find work, it is often of a casual, precarious and low-paid nature and they end up in the job/accommodation trap: namely, not being able to afford to pay for their own accommodation and only being able to take low-paid work so they can receive supplementary benefit and live in bed and breakfast.

The Irish Centre's own research project in 1985 underlined this fact. They followed up 250 young people a few weeks after arriving in London and found over 80 per cent still unemployed. Those in jobs were, in the main, holding down temporary poorly paid posts. Cara, the Irish Homeless and Rootless project, added to this picture in their survey in the same year. Fifty-seven per cent of their sample had not made any arrangements for accommodation before leaving Ireland. Twenty-seven per cent of that group had spent some time sleeping rough since their arrival, and these were usually likely to be the younger age group, fifteen years of age and upwards.

The worry that agencies have about the young Irish is that some will fall into the same trap as many of those in their forties and fifties who came to Britain in the 1950s and now are a large percentage of hostel dwellers. Many young people have little motivation to use local facilities and are reluctant to put their names forward for council housing. They are falling very rapidly into a state of mind that does not allow them to unpack their suitcase and put down roots. They see themselves as temporary dwellers, making enough money to enable them to return to Ireland with something behind them. They are difficult to motivate because 'home' is still seen as Ireland and no attempts are made to settle here.

There is concern about the percentage of young Irish people in homeless agencies and night shelters. The feeling is that there is nothing specific for this group. Many feel lost, culturally, in this society and as yet there is nowhere to go which could help them bridge that divide and meet their needs as young people. Anxiety has also been expressed about the presence of young Irish people in prostitution, the vulnerability to pimps of young girls arriving penniless off the trains and the increasing presence of young lads in the rent boy scene. For many an element of their entry into prostitution has to do with their displacement from their communities and the poverty within that community at home.

The needs
Agencies would like to see the development of a service that offers ongoing counselling and support to young people that would help them to make sense of their cultural origins and preserve them, while relating to what is essentially an alien way of life. This Irish dimension is important. Many young Irish people suffer similar feelings of alienation to other ethnic groups despite the fact that, as a nation, their presence may seem to be taken for granted. Irish young people are wary of agencies they see as only set up for English people and they are very reluctant to talk about those issues of their homelessness that have to do with family, marriage or sexuality, feeling that English workers will not understand their context.

The young Irish also have specific needs in terms of finding employment and being helped through the morass of difficulties around eligibility, social security and problem employers. Some young people end up in prison, many for DHSS-related crime. They have no one to visit them or give them the specific support they need while in prison and the care and attention necessary when they leave.

For all these reasons, workers are very concerned about the fate of the young Irish immigrant. They are particularly concerned that the particular dimensions of Irish homelessness should not be misunderstood or ignored when the facts about homelessness are presented. There is no little concern that the young Irish are increasingly becoming an oppressed ethnic minority, whose problems are hidden and unacknowledged in Britain.

7 Runaways and homelessness

'When life becomes unbearable for children they fade. They do not necessarily fall ill and die, but they fade in other ways. They create chaos, throw tantrums, provoke disharmony, divide their families, become loners, fail at school, they truant, they steal, they lie, they dabble in alcohol and drugs, and finally they run away from home.' (Stanislaus Kennedy, ed, *Streetwise. Homelessness among the Young in Ireland and Abroad.*)

The nature of the runaway

Leaving home is a complex process. For many young people it is a snap decision. They 'act' rather than 'reflect'. There is no doubt that this is very true of those young people for whom running away is an essential component of this process. Some would feel that the term 'running away' does not do justice to their courage in leaving behind situations and people that are intolerable. They feel the emphasis ought to be on 'running towards' that which offers a better and safer future.

Erica De'Ath of the Children's Society has written a great deal about the nature of such young people (De'Ath & Sparks 1986). For her the term 'runaways' encompasses missing children, absconders (especially from local authority care), the homeless and the rootless drifters. She defines a runaway as 'a young person, under seventeen years of age or in local authority care, who has either left home (or residential care) of his or her own accord, but without agreement, or is forced to leave and is missing for more than one night'. Susanna Agnelli (1986) describes them as 'street children' who 'live on the margins of the adult world . . . victims of alienation and systematic exclusion. Their lives are shaped by deprivation, violence and fear'. She describes some as being 'on the streets', that is, those who keep some links with their families, and others 'of the streets', those who are totally on their own. Their problems, according to De'Ath (1987), encompass homelessness, prostitution, shop lifting and begging and they are prey to disease, malnutrition, exploitation and violence.

Common to all runaways is the decision to run and stay away, because of the long-term conflict they have with parents or parent substitutes. Parental rejection is often as not coupled with school failure and a life that may include delinquency, drug abuse, the gang, physical hardships, a repressive institution and resignation to one's fate. Agnelli feels that the majority of street children in industrial countries are victims of 'inner-city decay, inherited deprivation, chronic unemployment, impossible housing markets, extraordinary high divorce rates and claustrophobic stress'. She sees little difference between street children in developing and industrial countries. She says they are all 'victims of the crisis of the family'. 'The breakdown of family structure and traditional values, massive emigration, the economic decline of neighbourhoods in the North and growing sophistication of cities in the South, are the factors that narrow the differences between streets in different continents.'

In many ways the street alienates youngsters from the mainstream of society. Certainly those who work with Black youngsters in London emphasise this fact. They feel written off by society with no place in its structure. So, as Agnelli says, they 'hold its standards in contempt' and 'consider its concern for property hypocritical'. The violence that is so often part and parcel of these young people's lives, both received and acted out, Agnelli sees as 'part of the language of deprivation' and 'no more than the logical consequence of the violence of which the youngster was a victim in the family'. For young Black people in Britain it is very much the consequence of the violence that continues to be done to them and their families by a society that knows little of their suffering and cares even less.

The size of the problem

As the title of Susanna Agnelli's book suggests, street children are a growing urban tragedy, but it is a tragedy which, of its nature, does not easily lend itself to be counted and quantified. According to official statistics, almost 3,000 young people were reported missing in the Metropolitan Police Area in 1985. De'Ath (1987) tells of twenty-seven police forces who listed 42,966 children reported missing in 1985, which she feels would suggest a national figure of between 75,000 and 85,000 each year. This does not take into account the fact that those missing for up to a few hours to less than a week do not have to be reported missing as such.

Shelter (NCH 1987) suggested a figure in 1985 of 80,000 cases of youth homelessness. This is not a definitive figure, but it is a clear indication of the problem. As Sereny (1984) suggests, a vast majority of young people return home after forty-eight hours. The Metropolitan Police indicate that up to 20,000 such youngsters are reported missing each year in their area, but records are not required to be kept if they return quickly enough. The problem is that many run repeatedly till eventually their parents give up recording them as missing. Sereny says that about 10 per cent of all runaways are never found, and there are clear indications that some parents are quite indifferent to their children being found or not. Because of their age and often the situations they have run from, young people are not easily found, as agencies in London would attest, though they would argue that the numbers of younger people, sixteen years of age and under, are on the increase.

The Central London Teenage Project, set up by the Children's Society to help young people who run away from home, have published statistics about the 271 young people who passed through the project in 1985/86 (Newman 1987). Sixty-two per cent had run from home, 37 per cent from local authority care, and 47 per cent of the latter had run at least five times. Seventeen per cent of all young people (25 per cent of all females, 8 per cent of all males) had been sexually abused, many females through rape or abuse by father or another male relative. The males had been abused by older men, usually after arriving in London.

Figures from the National Children's Homes (1987) suggest that the factors that contribute to young people running off are not diminishing in their intensity. One in five children are likely to see their parents divorcing before they reach the age of sixteen, and the numbers of children under five years of age of divorced parents are on the increase. In 1985 the report shows that of every one hundred divorcing couples in England and Wales, twenty-four had one child under sixteen years of age, twenty-three had two and eight had three or more—a national figure of over 160,000. It is estimated that there were 960,000 lone parents in 1985, one in five families in the London area alone. Over 1.25 million children live in families where the main breadwinner is unemployed, and in 1983 3.6 million parents and children were living in families where the level of income is below the poverty line. There is every belief according to the report, that 1987 figures will show an increase.

As with the dramatic increase in homelessness, there is no indication that the problem of young runaways is likely to diminish in the near future. Population projections according to the Office of Population Censuses and Surveys show a decrease in the number of children under sixteen years of age till 1988. After that numbers will increase until the year 2001. Half the world's population will be under twenty-five by that date, and in the five to nineteen age group Agnelli says there will be 247 million more urban children than today, the vast majority of whom will be in developing countries. Nevertheless, it is clear that the presence of young people in the cities of industrial countries is not likely to diminish and in Britain their plight is likely to become worse unless the trend towards inner city poverty and decay can be reversed.

Reasons for running

There are theories propounded that some young people choose to run because of some hereditary predisposition, no matter what home conditions are like. These theories suggest that the young are seeking greater freedom and autonomy and point to the fact that this group of young people show many positive qualities in their lives and are not the stereotyped dropouts of popular portrayals.

Be that as it may, most of those who work with young runaways point very clearly to the dynamics of family life as the main reasons. The common factor is one of a family in great crisis whose relationships, if not broken completely, are severely strained for a whole host of reasons. All too often the physical resources of the home may be so limited that the young feel they have to move out just to let the rest of the family have a better chance of living together. For others, divorce, the lack of a strong father figure, or the presence of an unacceptable step-parent may be the trigger. Unemployment in the family is a major cause as the young feel guilty at being kept in a family where they cannot pay their way and often their own parents may have been out of work for some time.

The pressures in such homes are often released through a violence which destroys the fragile relationships existing in the family. Often where one-parent families are trying to cope, the strain on one parent, usually the mother, is such that the close bonding between mother and child is affected, leaving the young emotionally scarred and insecure. For some, the absence of parents from the home in their formative years at times of the day when they were most needed, has led to the latch-key teenager who is alienated from the family, lacking those structures in his or her life that make for security and balanced development.

External structures do not offer the stability the young person seeks. Schools are often remote, alienating places that prepare young people for a world they can never hope to see and often ignore the realities they are trying to cope with on a daily basis. So they become centres of failure for some young people who reject them, often from a very early age. For others, schools are places to be feared as they suffer physical and emotional abuse from their peer group and a rejection in the classroom from their teachers who often do not have the expertise or the time to devote to their individual welfare.

For many in local authority, residential care, one unhappy home has been swapped for another. They feel trapped in a system that is socially isolating where nothing ever seems to happen for them, where staff come and go so quickly that relationships can only be superficial and transitory, where rules and restrictions appear punitive and where no one either asks them what they would like or listens to them when they plead to be heard. These young are unhappy and disillusioned and despair in the ability of the adult world ever to give them the care and security they crave for.

For some young people, running from home is an escape from sexual abuse that has often gone on from early childhood. The Central London Teenage Project found 17 per cent of those who attended their project between 1985/86 had suffered in this way and a study by Arlene McCormack and others (1986) in the USA found that 38 per cent of male and 73 per cent of female runaways reported being sexually abused. The authors felt that their study confirmed past findings that identified runaways as a high-risk group for sexual abuse.

Often the way back for those who run off is a difficult one. There are many cases where parents are relieved and happy when contact is made with them and the CLTP have found that many have wanted to improve their relationships with their offspring, though they needed a great deal of support themselves to do so (Brown 1987). For those young people who have been forced out of home, a return is often impossible. Robert Borgman's study (1986) found that ejecting children for impossible behaviour is likely to become a habitual response in a family and prone to become a permanent expulsion if the child goes back and plays up again. There are some indications that the involvement of close relatives on the child's behalf can effect reconciliation, though Borgman is unable to predict whether agency-instigated involvement with relatives would have the same effect.

For young people running from local authority care, a return to their residential base can often be a traumatic and unhelpful experience. The CLTP have experienced some difficulties and a lack of co-operation on the part of some social service departments who have appeared to be threatened by the attempts of the project to advocate on the youngsters' behalf and to get to the roots of the problem. For those who have been sexually abused, however, a return home is out of the question. Arlene McCormack and her team predict that sexually abused female runaways are significantly more likely than non-abused counterparts to engage in criminal and delinquent activities, and that though they are often reluctant to run from an abusive home situation, once they do, they are at high risk for repeated abuse.

Not much is available to these young people who cannot, or do not want to, return home. As has already been described, housing departments will offer them nothing. Education departments see them as dropouts, and, without education, employment in a highly competitive market is very unlikely. As Agnelli (1986) points out, 'the record of most countries recognising and tackling the issue is largely disappointing. Having been consistently avoided, it has grown to huge proportions before attracting the proper attentions. Authorities do the minimum and only under pressure'.

Conclusion

In many ways, those young people who run away have been failed both by their families and by the society in which they live. They are very much victims of our civilisation which stresses the material and the technological above basic human dignity.

Unless, as Agnelli and many others have stressed, society gives a greater recognition of and a more central place to the caring ethic, it runs the risk of creating a substantial alienated sub-culture, with no loyalties to their fellow citizens and even less respect for the culture and traditions they hold dear.

The plight of so many young people in Britain who are forced to leave home, often after years of physical and emotional torture, is a disturbing one and demands a caring response. But, as Agnelli stresses, 'this will not come about by sermons or wishful thinking: it must be actively nurtured'.

8 Young women and homelessness

'The obvious point is overlooked: if homelessness is largely evaluated by looking at the provision for homeless people, for as long as there are fewer beds for homeless women than men, there will appear to be fewer homeless women than homeless men. A vicious circle is perpetuated: the research justifies the lack of provision and the lack of provision predetermines the outcome of the research.' (Helen Austerberry and Sophie Watson, *Women on the Margin. A Study of Single Women's Housing Problems.*)

The situation in London

There is a general feeling that women are underrepresented in the West End and most agencies report taking in greater numbers of males rather than females (except where a quota system is set up). Staff feel they cannot be dogmatic as to why this is so, but overwhelmingly there is the feeling that young women have particular needs which are often not being met.

In Central London, figures will differ according to projects and their nature, but between 30 per cent and 40 per cent of those who use the services on average are women. Higher figures are noted in those projects which offer support to young Black people. Young Black women are not slow in coming forward to seek the help which is necessary for them and on average between 50 per cent and 60 per cent use the services available.

Central London is a harsh, demanding place that is hard for females to survive in. Many young women are frightened and can be put off by some of the provision that is available. It is generally felt that, to keep a roof over their heads, young women will tolerate far more difficult situations than their male peers. This is why, it is argued, young women are not as visible as young men on the homeless circuit, although some feel that this situation may be changing. This may partly be due to the fact that agencies have gone out of their way to make sure that what is offered can be taken up by young women, with emphasis on special days for women, women's groups and space set aside for women only. On the other hand, young women may be becoming less tolerant of their hidden homelessness and be more demanding of existing services.

In general it is felt that young women worry far more about homelessness than young men. They have every reason to do so, because it is clear they are far more at risk of emotional and sexual exploitation than male peers. They want to get out of their situations quickly and yet they won't accept some provision just for the sake of it.

Young women have to go to places, asking for help, where men are in the majority. Some have suffered sexual abuse, physical violence and personal degradation at the hands of men, so walking into units that have large numbers of male residents and staff takes a particular kind of courage. It is true that places for young women are more readily available, though some are unacceptable to them. Large hostels or dormitory-style accommodation are hard for them to cope with and they prefer smaller-type provision that allows for less sharing and more single rooms. This range of accommodation is not readily available, though to be fair not all young women necessarily want accommodation apart from young men. Many resent it if young men are kept out because of women's days, or special women's groups. Some young women do link up with young men because they can provide security from some of the harassment of the homeless circuit.

The need for security
It is this security that workers feel young women ask for continuously. They need provision that allows them privacy with physical and emotional safety. They are often more mature than their male counterparts. This may be because the decision to move away from home has been much harder and may have been weighed up more carefully, so a young woman knows what to expect and is clear what she wants. Certainly this is very true of young women from ethnic minorities. They are not prepared to tolerate anything less than what they know they need. Other young women are intolerant of hostels and hostel rules and cope better with smaller more flexible provision. Workers feel that seventeen-year-olds especially can be quite hard to motivate, yet they too demand a secure base to help them cope.

An aspect of this security for young women has to do with their need for time and space to sort themselves out, without challenge from others and without the fear of having to move on before they

are ready to do so. Some have come from homes that have been small and overcrowded and have felt pressurised into moving out. To swap that situation for a similar one in an agency where space is at a premium is an option that many young women won't take up. That is why some are prepared to sleep on a friend's floor and others will move in with male friends, feeling that even the vagaries of that set up can offer more in the short term than the homeless circuit.

There is also no doubt that some young women need particular services especially some direct access, women-only, provision that can offer immediate respite, counselling and an opportunity to come to terms with their immediate situation. Safe houses that are free of male domination and allow those young women who need protection from males a secure haven are sadly lacking. This is particularly so for some young women who are on drugs and who are into prostitution as a way of paying for their habit. The opportunity to come off drugs and to break their dependence on prostitution will be affected by their ability to escape from their pimps.

Young women and prostitution
There is evidence that once young women have become heavily involved in the prostitution scene it may be almost impossible for them to come off. The task is to try to prevent them getting into

the life in the first place, because, once in, they become part of a particular subculture with its own norms and peer pressure. They live in a twilight-type world that is so far removed from the everyday that they are frightened to opt out of the 'security' that it offers them. If such young women have entered the life of prostitution as a way out of their homelessness, they find it that much more difficult to move away from it. Basically the money is too good and this outweighs the dangers of staying in.

The girls themselves argue that prevention is far better than cure and that young girls have a better chance if they are helped early on. Workers tell of some young girls being helped in this way by older prostitutes who will 'shop' them to the police for their own good, or in some cases have clubbed together to collect the fare to send them back home. There is no doubt that this 'altruism' is largely motivated by the threat a young girl makes to the business of established, older prostitutes, but it is also clear that in some cases the concern for the individual's good is quite genuine.

Police activity in known areas and the closure of many of the Soho clubs have certainly cut back on the visibility of female prostitution in Central London. Much of it has been driven out to the suburbs or inside into a variety of 'specialised' agencies. This makes it all the more difficult for young women to be offered support to move away from this lifestyle. Some argue that specialist provision to help such young women needs to be set up as an act of good faith. It is notoriously difficult for young people to escape this lifestyle and only by offering provision that is secure and welcoming can that process be initiated.

Pregnant young women

Without exception, workers lament the lack of any provision to care for homeless young women who are pregnant. They are very difficult to cope with within existing provision because of their specialist needs and many have to declare themselves as of no fixed abode to get local authorities to act. The saddest effect of this is that it allows a young woman to be homeless, rootless, full of uncertainty, with no security at a time in her life when personal safety and security and a settled base are essential for her own emotional development and the well being of her unborn child. It is one thing to face the uncertainties of single parenthood as a teenager, but to do so from bed and breakfast with few supports and little idea of what the future holds or where 'home' will be must be intolerable and must have long-term detrimental effects on the emotional well-being of mother and child. Provision for these young people is long overdue.

Young women and drugs
Some young women live the life of a prostitute in order to support the drug habits of their male friends or partners. So moving away from this life has additional difficulties attached. Those young women with children face the same dilemma and are also very much at risk. They are afraid to approach drug agencies in case statutory services remove their children from them because of their drug habits and until very recently no provision for treating women with children was available. In general, this problem faces young women in their twenties rather than the teenage group.

Statutory provision
Those young women of sixteen and seventeen years of age who come into contact with social services or probation are not likely to receive a great deal of help. Certainly social services are faced with the dilemma of doing something for those almost seventeen because of the problems of trying to effect statutory support. A young girl's age, plus her refusal to be helped by statutory services, often mean social services' hands are effectively tied.

Finding places for sixteen- to seventeen-year-olds in probation hostels is a demanding task. They are such a difficult group that agencies are very reluctant to help them. It seems the Probation Service will not refer young women of that age.

There is some evidence that a substantial minority of those held in police cells on bail awaiting places in Holloway are seventeen-year-old young women for whom there is no provision. Some workers feel that it is at this point that young women may be most receptive to help and support, especially those who come before the courts on charges of soliciting. The need, it seems, is over-whelming. Home Office money is becoming available again, yet so far no-one has taken up the challenge of meeting the needs of these young women.

Other problems facing young women
Various other difficulties facing young homeless women have also been highlighted by the agencies. Some have to leave their home

and home areas because they are unacceptable as lesbians and
are very much in need of security and understanding. There is
also some evidence of mental illness, and little provision for such
people in existing agencies. Discrimination in employment and
lack of job security in the service industry as waitresses and
barmaids are common factors.

Intimidation and harassment from landlords can be quite
common just because they are females. Some has been seen in
DHSS offices which, in a few cases, have required that young
women report for payment on a daily basis, effectively depriving
them of the opportunity both to find and secure accommodation.
To be young, homeless and female in London requires courage
that would test the most emotionally secure individual and many
feel that the plight of such young women is a sad commentary
on our society and a clear indication just how far we need to go
to remove the discrimination that exists.

Conclusion

Some workers feel that this situation exists because there is a lack
of research and publicity about the needs of such young women.
It is argued that homelessness has too often been seen as a male
preserve and that support structures are male-orientated and male-
dominated. There is no doubt that stringent efforts have been
made to change this in existing agencies, but it is still argued that
the will to help this group plus the financial resources are still
sadly lacking, particularly in statutory services. The fact that
women are prepared to tolerate difficult circumstances masks the
extent of the problem and contributes, no doubt, to the scarcity
of specific accommodation services.

There is a clear need to give young women security, space and
time to make decisions about their future. There is some criticism
of statutory services for placing so many of them in care because
they are in moral danger. This, it is argued, does little for them
and certainly does not address their long-term needs, because
those who leave care and are homeless stand out as being the most
difficult to help and the most incapable of coping. In the long term,
prevention is far better than cure and workers feel it is only this
type of approach that can offer these young people the help they
require.

9 Young people and drugs

'Drug use is most likely to be converted into severe drug-related problems when it occurs in the context of an extended biography involving housing, employment and attendant problems.' (Nicholas Dorn and Nigel South, *Helping Drug Users.*)

'It does not follow that all problem drinkers are homeless because of their drinking. It is, however, reasonable to suggest that if drink is not always an initial cause of home-lessness, it is a major factor which keeps individuals homeless.' (The Central London Outreach Team, *Sleeping Out in Central London.*)

For some young people, drugs and alcohol are a significant aspect of their homelessness. The numbers of such young people are not clear, but a Scottish Health Education Report in 1986 emphasised that homelessness is but one of many other factors that contribute to a high proportion of young drug casualties. For many in their teens and twenties, this report asserts, drugs are taken for their curiosity value. For others they are used to relieve stress. The temptation to do this when a young person is alone and rootless can be almost overwhelming, and once hooked on drugs or alcohol the chances of escaping from the homeless circuit are greatly reduced.

Drugs—a social issue

At an international youth forum in Wales in July 1985, a certain Rick Little, founder of the Quest National Centre in Colombus, Ohio, began his speech by declaring that, 'We don't have a drug, alcohol or sex problem—we have a people problem'. It is an important distinction. Drug taking is a social problem. As Holroyd notes, 'It does not occur just in units or hospitals. It happens in estates, in neighbourhoods and in people's homes' (Holroyd 1986).

For regular drug users, the drug scene itself involves work and gives a sense of security and excitement which is missing in their immediate environment. They have to develop and maintain a routine of contacts and acquire, pass on and exchange knowledge about availability of drugs, their prices and supply. Thus the users are enmeshed in a supportive social network whose members are busy keeping one another busy. A purpose now exists in their lives where none did before, no matter how negatively this may be viewed by their family and non-drug-using friends. It is no wonder that in many cases the drug itself is not as important as the lifestyle associated with it, and to come off drugs successfully the young people have to reconstruct their lives around non-drug activities and relationships.

The drug user
Who then is at risk? A research study by the DHSS in 1986 examined seven groups to see how they varied in terms of being exposed to and therefore at risk from contact with drugs. The group most likely to be at risk was those who were bored with life, in conflict with their parents and anti-establishment. They were people who looked for excitement and accepted that risk must be a necessary part of living. They were pro-smoking and pro-drinking but were also the group that was likely to be above average in employment. This contrasts with the Scottish Health Education Group (1986) who, while agreeing that those deeply involved with drugs were those more likely to be estranged from their families, disagreed that they were likely to be those in work. They would see this group as having little stake in the daily world of work.

A growing proportion of drug addicts are women, especially young women with children. The latter are more at risk because they hold back from presenting themselves for treatment or even advice in case their children are taken into care. Others are being turned away because the agencies cannot get funding. It is for this reason that the City Road Drug Project in Islington intends to open up a unit for women and their children and why Phoenix House was due to open its Family Unit in May 1987.

In a study published in 1986 (Pritchard et al 1986), drug misusers among fourth and fifth formers at school were likely to have higher levels of father unemployment, parents absent from the home, and be part of a large family. They were also likely to be significantly associated with under-age drinking, vandalism, truancy, fighting and smoking. But it was the impact of unemployment that the authors were particularly concerned with. Its relation to drugs and the young is not clearly understood, but studies of young heroin users found a higher than expected rate of unemployment and those who went on to misuse drugs after leaving school were more likely to be unemployed (Institute for the Study of Drug Dependence 1986).

Drug takers are not a homogeneous group and the reasons why individuals start to take drugs, continue on them, and why some successfully come off them will vary from one person to another. Dr John Strang said drug addiction might well not be a condition but a form of disturbance or behaviour associated with a wide range of origins (Strang 1984). Mark Lee found that established users largely had problems around drug use, health and legal difficulties. The less established users and drug-free group were more likely to be experiencing problems about accommodation, unemployment and family relationships (Lee 1987). Hence the importance of concentrating on the individual and his or her problem and of offering a range of interventions and responses.

Strang used the term 'problem drug taker' whom he described as 'someone who experiences physical, psychological, social or legal problems as a result of his or her intoxication and/or regular excessive consumption and/or dependence on a drug or drugs'. He felt this definition encouraged a broader consideration of the problem. Others have indicated that drug-related difficulties are indications of deeper problems around housing, money, health, relationships and legal difficulties.

Mark Lee gave a fairly detailed description of the Central London drug user. He found that few were in regular contact with their families and only the fifteen- to nineteen-year-old group were likely to be living in the parental home. Most were of working- and lower-middle-class backgrounds and 85 per cent were unemployed. Many supplemented their income through begging, prostitution, shoplifting or by selling part of their own drug supply. Thirteen per cent had criminal records and one in ten had outstanding legal problems at time of contact.

There is no doubt that some users, particularly among the young, take drugs for pleasure, for experiments and to pass the time. However, this use becomes serious when it occurs in the context of an extended biography of housing problems, employment difficulties, homelessness and social and personal handicap.

Lee found that most users lived by a strict, though unwritten, set of social rules and conventions. Included among these were not giving someone their first fix, not selling to non-dependent drug users and not encouraging the latter to use substances. About a fifth of all users Lee met were notified as users to the Home

Office, in broad agreement with national trends. The vast majority of young drug users, however, had never been involved with a specialist drug agency and were not in touch with any of the helping agencies in the Central London area.

Some of these young people may well have entered the world of hard drugs through solvent abuse. A recent article suggested that 13 per cent of solvent abusers, especially solitary abusers, turn to hard drugs (Gay 1986). Some may also be involved in crime. American literature highlights drug users as participants in crime, fencing, pimping and prostitution (Manning and Redlinger 1983). Studies have found that drug use may lead to crime, but the reverse may also be the case, or that both crime and drugs may be caused by a third factor (ISDD 1986). However, especially for young drug users, it is clear that crime is committed for the sole purpose of getting money to finance a habit (House of Commons 1985).

The size of the problem
In the United Kingdom
Home Office figures show a trebling in the numbers of all those taking notifiable drugs since the late seventies. Michael Meacher, the former Shadow Health Minister, said that the official 1983 figure of 10,000 addicts was at considerable odds with the findings of a Drug Indicators Project which found five unidentified drug takers for every identified user in the communities examined (Meacher 1984). The Committee on the Misuse of Drugs quotes 40,000 users. Professor Malcolm Lauder of the Maudsley assumes 100,000 as a conservative figure, but says the real figure could be 250,000. A 1985 DHSS report showed that the number of addicts notified by doctors to the Chief Medical Officer at the Home Office was a rising trend—42 per cent up in 1983, and 28 per cent up in 1984. Those receiving in-patient treatment had gone up 76 per cent on the 1979 figure. This report would agree with the assertion in Michael Meacher's book that notified addicts represent a five-fold underestimate of actual users. Particular areas could differ even more and the report points to a 1981 study in Scotland in one area that estimated a notification rate of only one in ten.

In London
Figures in 1983 of resident addicts from the North West Thames area, representing a fifth of all United Kingdom notifications, lead

the area to believe that the problem of drug misuse continues to grow. Police records in the metropolitan area show 1,813 new addicts in 1983 and between 1984 and 1985 the London drug projects dealt with 4,623 addicts.

However, these figures give no indication of the nature of the problem or its severity among young people. Mark Lee's study of young drug users in Central London gives a much better indication of trends. Part of his task led him to look at sixteen youth agencies in Camden and Westminster. These agencies dealt with an age range from seven- to twenty-five-year-olds, though the predominant group for most projects was the fifteen to nineteen group. These groups were mainly White and Afro-Caribbean, predominantly male, of whom roughly a third were employed, a third unemployed and the remainder too young for employment. An average of 1,892 people used the agencies each week. Of these 25 per cent were suspected of using drugs and 19 per cent were known users. The highest prevalence of drug use was in agencies serving the fifteen- to eighteen-year-old age group.

Lee's own work covers the period from July 1985 to December 1986, when as a sole detached worker at the Hungerford Project he attempted to make contact with drug users in Central London, particularly the young. His work showed that he was more successful in contacting them, and particularly young women, than office-based agencies. Sixty per cent of those he saw were from in and around London, 10 per cent came from the Home Counties and 30 per cent came from London and the South East. Forty-five per cent of this latter group were living in temporary accommodation and 14 per cent had no fixed abode. Of the total sampled, one-third were part of the transient youth community in Central London, one-third were 'local visitors', that is from London and the South East. The rest were either indigenous to Central London or else their exact location was not known. Thirty-seven per cent were aged nineteen or under and a further 27 per cent were aged between twenty and twenty-two. These figures bear comparison with those in the previous paragraph and would suggest that a substantial minority of young people in Central London, that is those aged nineteen and under, may be involved in drugs in some way, and that a substantial minority of those will be in temporary accommodation or of no fixed abode.

Alcohol

There is an argument that says that all the concern about drug abuse has ignored the effects of the most deadly drug of all—alcohol (Steele 1986). Dr Bruce Ritson (1987) claims that alcohol-related problems run in families and that sons of problem drinkers are four times more likely to develop drinking problems themselves. The children of such families, he argues, mature at a very early age, have trouble developing relationships and are prey to a variety of neuroses in later life. The Central London Outreach Team (1984) have clearly pointed out that if drink is not the initial cause of homelessness, then it is a major factor which keeps individuals homeless.

Drugs and homelessness

A lot of young people who use drugs may have an unsettled lifestyle, but not necessarily a homeless one. However, for those who are on drugs, particularly heavy drugs, the chances of being homeless are quite high. The problem lies in trying to get a foothold in the housing market. Those who have drug- or alcohol-related problems often suffer ill health when there is nowhere to keep safe, warm and dry, nowhere to regard as home. Linked to this is the problem of maintaining a balanced diet when money is in short supply.

Without a settled base it is extremely difficult either to get a job or hold one down—and so the pattern continues. Without somewhere to call home, a young addict coming off a de-toxification programme will find it hard to remain drug free. Not too many hostels are willing to take those with a drug problem and give them the support necessary to survive.

Coping with the drugs problem

Policies

Ritson deplores the lack of guidelines on the treatment of alcohol problems and the lack of provision for those addicted. Although there have been clearer guidelines for the provision of drug abuse, much is still to be done.

The House of Commons Social Services Committee found that few local authorities had any idea as to how to deal with the social problem of drugs, few felt obliged to take any initiatives and many saw it as either a medical or criminal problem (Holroyd 1986).

Yet since 1970 and especially since 1978 the number of young people using opiates regularly, especially heroin, has risen ten-fold and the drug market has become more organised with close links to organised crime (Hartnoll 1986). The House of Commons Social Services Committee warned in 1985 that the full conse-quences of the incidences of heroin misuse in the eighties would not become visible for five or ten years. In the meantime so many of the young are in danger of becoming expendable cannon fodder.

If drug abuse is to be seen as a social problem, then ways of working with it must have a wider social context. Elizabeth Dun (1987) talks of an 'imaginative jump' being necessary to focus on 'the problem rather than the individual'. In this way workers can understand the meaning of what is happening to a client at any time. She says a balance has to be found early on between support and confrontation to help the individual come to terms with the disharmony in his or her life and disregard for self. The aim of the worker should be to ask the individual what he or she can do to facilitate change and help the addict put his or her life back together again. The worker will be more effective in this, according to Strang, if a crisis-response methodology can be developed, which takes into account the fluctuating motivation of the addict and helps him or her achieve 'a more stable and durable resolve to change'.

Treating the drug problem in itself will not produce change. It is necessary to go deeper and get at the social, economic, cultural and psychological problems that lie beneath (Jamieson *et al* 1984). Caution is necessary, however, if this is to be successful. Dun feels that any addict with a long history of instability and a short history of drug abuse will probably be using drugs to deal with anxiety. Anything that increases that anxiety will be counter-productive. If an individual does manage to come off drugs, then this anxiety will be unmasked. The danger of a relapse is quite likely, unless support systems are in place to help.

For those who have been using drugs since their early teens, whose whole life has been built around getting and using drugs, coming off drugs has other implications. For this group emotional development will have been arrested and they will need to pass through the growing-up stage of the teenage years before they can move out to find a place in the community. This is not an easy task and Dun urges workers to see themselves as helping individuals to come off drugs rather than appear to punish them for being on them. It is essential that recovering addicts be helped to see themselves and their world differently and build structures into their lives that will enable them to engage in activities that are not drug related.

Practice
To do all this successfully, it goes without saying that the addict needs to be engaged and helped at the time when he or she feels most in need. To this end Dorn (1985) calls for a national network of street agencies and Jamieson (1984) underlines the need for services that respond quickly and immediately and which do not erect barriers to entry.

Mark Lee (1987) has shown that outreach services are first of all necessary to provide information to users about the functions and availability of the agencies concerned and to give immediate help and intervention. After this initial contact they can be more easily referred to office-based and residential services, because initial fear and reluctance will have been overcome. To help this process he feels that agencies should provide clear and accurate information to their target groups. He also believes in the need for non-specialist youth and accommodation agencies to provide a comprehensive and appropriate service response to drug users. This is why Michael Meacher (1984) has called for a comprehensive service which is not unduly bureaucratic and which provides a variety of facilities and entry points. Without this Meacher fears little progress will be made in the treatment and rehabilitation of drug users.

The needs of women should receive particular consideration. A joint call from the DHSS, the Department of Education and Science (the DES), the Home Office and the Manpower Services Commission (the MSC) in December 1985 called for agencies to take account of the rising trend of female hard drug users, in particular the numbers of young female addicts, some of whom have children or are pregnant. And the Central London Outreach Team (1984) asked for the needs of homeless women with serious drink problems to be made a priority in any future provision.

Staffing
A comprehensive service however, should not overlook an essential component—well-trained staff. The DHSS and others (1985) said that the demand for specialist drug staff cannot but grow and

it has been one of Mark Lee's strongest pleas that training be given to all those who have to deal, in whatever way, with the young addicts. His research showed that 69 per cent of youth workers felt the need for training on drugs and drug-related issues, including emergency care. Half of those interviewed needed basic information on substances and symptoms recognition, while 44 per cent did not have enough basic information on the availability and functioning of existing specialist services. Lee is adamant that the potential for youth work with drug users, in terms of education, prevention and early intervention is considerable.

Conclusion

The plea that Mark Lee makes has been echoed in a wider sense in specialist reports. The Social Services Committee in Parliament said in 1985 that the main problems in the whole area of treatment and rehabilitation seemed to be a lack of co-ordination and general direction. It stressed the absence of research into and evaluation of past or present experience. That is why the response document to the report called for a more consciously directed research effort from the Advisory Council on the Misuse of Drugs. Dorn (1985) sees part of this task being carried out by street agencies. He suggested they should gather information and act as a pressure group for change. This information could also influence practice, give a better understanding of client need and create different options as a result.

Local authorities have also been urged to play their part in this work. The government response to the Social Services Committee stressed that drug abuse was as much a social as a medical problem, and the report of the Central London Outreach Team called for a shift in emphasis from an abuse approach to one that considers housing need, employment, personal relationships and access to Community Resources. All this is eloquently summed up by Ann Jamieson and her team: 'The translation of private troubles into public issues needs to be made over and over again. To recognise that vulnerability to drug dependence is in many cases caused by social conditions over which the individual has little control, especially unemployment and social deprivation. That the responsibility for dealing with individual inadequacies and alienation is a social not an individual one. That emotional difficulties, which at present are seemingly endemic in personal relationships, can be helped by care and therapy, but that present policies and practices actually tend either to neglect the struggles of children, young persons and adults in families or communities or even make things worse by the form of intervention practised. That people have been damaged and continue to be damaged by the way in which others treat them, sometimes by the harshness of their families towards them and sometimes by the failure of others to help those families cope with the pressures they have to face. The lack of services, in general, inevitably produces more people in special need' (Jamieson 1984).

10 Young people and prostitution

'No child in prostitution wants to be a prostitute. They long to be wanted—as children. They long to be loved. They long to be children.' (Gitta Sereny, *The Invisible Children: Child Prostitution in America, Germany and Britain.*)

'Our lives are in turmoil . . . we're caught between the childhood we never had and our false expectations of our fast approaching adulthood. At this confusing point in our lives, we're exposed . . . and we're easy prey.' (Debbie Kardon and Abby Lazar, *Easy Prey.*)

Introduction
For some young people the move away from home is as a consequence of sexual abuse. The literature has usually associated this reaction with females. However, as McCormack (1986) and others assert, while female runaways are more often victims of familial sexual abuse, male victims are more likely to make attempts to run away from abusive situations. Subsequently, males and females may find it difficult in later life to form relationships or maintain those in existence.

It is against this background that some young people leave home, become part of the homeless circuit, may also become part of the drug scene and eventually enter the world of prostitution. Many young people, according to McMullan (1987), would deny that they are prostitutes and would prefer to use the terms 'business girl/boy', 'rent boy', 'hustler' or 'trade'. They would define prostitution as an activity or a behaviour. McMullan would see it not so much as a commercial activity, but as a link in a chain of abuse, to which young people are in danger of becoming sexually and psychologically dependent. Because of this, he would argue that the notion that pimps wait at every mainline railway and bus station in London to ensnare and convert the young to a life of prostitution is an exaggerated one. He argues that it does happen, but not so frequently as one would like to believe, and where it does, the pimps are often preaching to the converted (1988).

The nature of those into prostitution

The definition of a young person involved in prostitution goes far beyond the simplistic description of a commercial activity. McMullan (1988) argues that it is a complex notion and has described at some length some of the characteristics concomitant to those who engage in this activity.

They are likely to be homeless and rootless, lacking in social skills, with a poor self-image having had little or no work experience. Some will have a criminal record and they will often have little idea how to claim money which they are usually very short of. As has been stated, many will have been abused in early life and will often set themselves up for continuing or further abuse. They will have left school early with no qualifications. They will have become exposed to a deviant sub-culture, be emotionally disturbed and have problems about their own identity. Many will have no idea why they entered prostitution and claim need for money as a reason for continuing in it.

These young people will be distrustful of male adults, whether they themselves are male or female. They are likely to be defensively aggressive, and use their sexual charm to get what they want. They will like to be seen as sexually active and sophisticated, but in reality will probably be quite the opposite. They are young people who will become easily frustrated when they have to deal with difficult situations and are likely to be out of touch with their personal power and potential. Yet Sereny (1984) adds, that contrary to what one might expect, they are mostly above-average children in every sense. She found them intelligent, imaginative, warm, curious and loving—very much individuals with a very special need for freedom.

Reasons for prostitution

Defined as a commercial activity, prostitution is the sale of sexual favours for money. A simplistic interpretation as to why young people end up 'on the game' might stop at that level. However, there is the issue about individual freedom and objective choice as to whether a young person knowingly and freely enters a particular way of life. When anyone makes a choice to do something, that choosing will be directed and largely dictated by previous choices. If these have been limited, then future choices will also be restricted, to the extent that individuals can often find themselves in situations which offer only one way out.

These are the issues that lead McMullan (1988) to state that the individual acts subjectively rather than objectively: he argues that the individual's entry to prostitution is consequent on sexual abuse. Only a minority, he argues, choose objectively to enter the life of a prostitute.

Part of the previous experience of young people will have to do with their inability to compete in a commercial world. Unemployment and a lack of occupational choice will have been determined by educational experiences that will often have left the individual both without qualifications and without the confidence and belief in self necessary to compete. For young women especially, with the burden of competing in what is still a male-dominated economy, the task is far greater. For those who find themselves with children in particular, their poverty determines that their sex is probably the most saleable commodity they have and is often the only way to give their children the basics of life. For some young people drugs have been so much part of their life that large sums of money obtained through prostitution are needed to sustain the habit. Often the basic insecurity of their lives will be increased by accommodation that is temporary or unsuitable, so increasing their fears and further isolating them in their communities.

For so many young people, the life of prostitution has been preceded by a history of continual and profound family conflict. Eventually they have been forced out of a home that has abused them physically, sexually and psychologically, and sometimes, as Sereny (1984) points out, with a brutality that has, often in subtle pathological ways, been sexually prompted. For others the family home is ruled by ambition and a possessiveness of them, or by parents who are cold and inhibited to an abnormal extent. Children, losing faith in their parents, fight them until the pain of the conflict becomes too great to bear and they run away.

McMullan (1987) highlights this as a process of abuse which results in the individual having what he terms 'a poorly experienced and underdeveloped sense of personal power'. This leads to deep feelings about being inconsequential to anyone or anything and creates a sense of helpless anger, exhibited in violence and depression. Add to this, the individual's lack of economic power, and McMullan argues that there is a legitimating force for a life of prostitution. Young people will argue that they 'do it for money' and that hides the abuse which McMullan argues is the motivating condition.

Sereny would agree with that and, like McMullan, highlights the taboo surrounding the abuse which may often remain a secret for many years, often because the individual abused has colluded with the abuser to do so. This linked to the individual's poor self-image and loathing of self, creates a vicious circle which is so hard to break. This is why McMullan feels that for some young people the 'life' of prostitution becomes a slow and self-torturing form of suicide.

He adds that prostitution gives and partially satisfies the young person's specific taste both of and for power. This power, the ability to influence and sometimes control one's environment, is part of the 'game'. But it is a game that can never be won and the paradox is that the young person is very likely to be in great danger. The denial of this danger by the young person puts them even more at risk.

Sereny argues that the 'game' is made possible by society's false sense of priority and responsibility. For society colludes in a game that allows young people to sell their bodies for money when they are thrown out of their families, who have the primary duty to care and cherish them. The collusion continues, according to Sereny, in the courts of the land that deliver minimal sentences to child abusers, rapists, and those who control young people for sexual and immoral purposes.

Secondly, she argues that our society has an additional responsibility in that it bombards the young through the media with artificial stimulation, forcing them into adult behaviour and into making decisions about everything under the sun, especially sex. The media present young people with images of sex that have little to do with reality. Sereny argues that too many young people are unable to absorb all of this, come to terms with it and make sense of it, without being damaged. In this way we limit the power of young people to choose.

The size of the problem

Young people enter prostitution at an early age. A research project by the Home Office in Holloway prison among fifty prostitute women found that the median age of entering prostitution was seventeen years and the age of the youngest entry was as low as twelve years (Duggan 1984). MacNamara and Karmen's study (1983) among young boys put the average age of first prostitutional activity at fourteen. The most unstable in the Home Office group were those who began before the age of sixteen.

These young people are likely to come from families that are in conflict, are unstable and where physical, sexual and psychological abuse is prevalent. The 1984 Home Office study showed 50 per cent leaving home because of rows and violence, and 16 per cent coming from homes described as 'violent'. MacNamara and Karmen report that 55 per cent of their group suffered physical abuse in the home. Two-thirds of the sixty-nine young people spoken to by Sereny admitted being disciplined at an early age with whips and canes. The Home Office Study showed 24 per cent who began prostitution before the age of sixteen had lost one or both parents at an early age.

Incest and sexual abuse in the home are also a common factor. McMullan (1987) quotes a Silbert and Pines study of 200 prostitutes that found 60 per cent abused as juveniles. Almost 70 per cent of that abuse was carried out by natural fathers or father figures

and the average age of the abused child was ten years. In MacNamara and Karmen's study 25 per cent had their first sexual experience with a relative while 17 per cent of Sereny's group admitted sexual abuse at home. Four per cent of the Home Office study admitted incestuous relationships with their fathers. Ninety per cent of the Silbert and Pines group attributed their entry into prostitution to the sexual abuse suffered largely at home, while most of the women in the Home Office study had been introduced to the work by women friends. Twelve per cent had been introduced by men, often in the context of violence.

Thirty per cent of the women in the Home Office group started prostituting because of a severe need of cash. Seventy per cent of the group had been unemployed for a long time. But the common factor for both girls and boys is a history of trauma and abuse suffered from early childhood.

Society does little to help. Girls found prostituting are fined while boys are often sent for psychiatric reports—a clear case, according to McMullan, of male's perception of a female's place in the world! The young people themselves 'feel valueless in a world of adults who cannot help them, and valueless as sons and daughters of parents whose lives, they are convinced, they hinder rather than enrich' (Sereny 1984).

Responses to young people in prostitution

Ritchie McMullan (1987) is clear that prostitution is a moral issue to be worked through. However, he makes a plea that we should not make moral judgements of a young person who has already been seriously damaged in life, because of the danger of that young person coming to own that identification more fully. For a young person involved in some form of prostitution to be called a prostitute may lead them to accept that they are 'bad', 'no good' and deserving of the term. McMullan would prefer that we see young people both as victims, because of the sexual abuse to them in their lives, and as victimisers because they trick their clients by stealing from them or making them pay more. Fundamentally, however, these young people are people with great needs which can and ought to be met.

In the same article, McMullan argues that we need to help the young abused person free him or herself from the role of victim. Child abuse, he argues, is in reality an adult abuse of power over the child. Young people need to know this and so free themselves from the guilt so many feel that, somehow, they were responsible for the abuse. McMullan argues that it is up to the adult abuser to stop abusing. It is he or she who is responsible, not the child.

Third, McMullan argues that as young people do not choose freely to enter prostitution, they cannot be expected freely to give up that way of living. Sereny agrees. She says this escape can rarely be achieved by the young people on their own and often will be brought about only as a result of injury, illness, a particular traumatic event or some combination of all three.

For Sereny, one of the phenomena of youth prostitution is the fact that adults, generally speaking, don't want to know, and parents least of all. They go to great extremes to avoid knowing. For many of these parents, Sereny found that the basic issue was that they had no idea how to be parents. They had never been taught the skills and often were completely ignorant of basic issues. Common to both boys and girls was the lack of attention paid to them by their parents and their ignorance of the suffering of their children either in school or in general outside the home.

Young people involved in prostitution do realise that their value as children, their rights to be protected and cared for have been cruelly taken away from them. They feel worthless and of no use to anyone. Prostitution, Sereny argues, is an act of extreme self-abasement on their behalf. She argues that the young understand this aspect of their lives very clearly and that it serves both to feed their contempt of themselves and to express the anger, fear and helplessness which they feel against those who caused it—their parents.

Needs of young people in prostitution

The world of prostitution is but one aspect of the lives of some of those who are homeless and at risk. Workers argue that efforts must be made to set up and co-ordinate services in the home areas of those who run, so support can be given to them at the time when they are most vulnerable and most in need. In particular in this context they stress that young women's needs in terms of housing, welfare benefits, child care and access to legal advice must be looked at and particular efforts made to help them into training, education and employment.

Those who work with these young people must be given appropriate training so they can help them understand and make sense of their lives and enable them to widen their prospective choices. Erica De'Ath (1987) would like to see that undertaken in residential care especially. She wants to ensure that young people are listened to, are involved in all aspects of planning and negotiation of the next steps in their lives and participate in case reviews. She wants to see a complaints procedure and appropriate guidance and counselling available for them.

Sereny (1984) says that the young people she writes about demonstrated a 'desperate need for family life, for structure in their environment and for the kind of support found in a faith or in some degree of intellectual discipline'. Unless the family context of young people who enter prostitution is acknowledged and unresolved family issues are highlighted and worked through, justice will not begin to be done to the needs of these young people. A family therapy/systemic approach needs to be adopted in projects and in particular specific feelings of self loathing need to be addressed and worked through. Maria Duggan's work highlighted the views of some older prostitutes who felt there was a need for an outreach programme which could make contact with younger women, especially newcomers to the street, and give them the sympathetic and skilled work needed at a time when they had the most potential for change.

Many young people have great fears about leaving a life of prostitution, despite the dangers and difficulties of staying on. Duggan found that the lack of support structure to create a new way of life was the biggest fear to be overcome. For those who are entrenched in the life, that very entrenchment becomes the reason for staying in it. For when they tried to seek advice, even on issues that had nothing to do with prostitution, the stigma of being a prostitute prevented them from making that step forward.

McMullan (1987) is clear that only the young person in prostitution can and should decide when he or she is ready to come out of it. The worker can facilitate this by helping the individual acknowledge the true, good, strong self within and reflect back to that good person the image of the false self. If the individual can distinguish them, then he or she will go a long way towards facilitating the good strong person within. The worker has to help the individual build up courage and confidence so his or her own self image can be 'healed enough to move towards positive self-change'.

However, to help young people make those moves, Maria Duggan feels strongly that we have to challenge 'sexist, racist and class ridden social structures and the ideology that supports them at a very deep level'. Rehabilitation of prostitutes she finds to be a difficult task in a climate that shifts the emphasis from under-lying social reasons for prostitution on to the individual who is labelled as 'different' from all other men and women.

Conclusion

Young people who have been in prostitution, as McMullan (1987) says, need to be put back in touch with their personal power and positive potential. One of the saddest comments in Sereny's book came from a young prostitute, Nell. She saw herself as 'little more than a carrier bag from a shop—once used, that's that'. It is the emotional strain that young people feel—not what they feel to their clients, but to themselves—that causes the most pain, and the sense that something precious, home and childhood, has been lost, perhaps for ever. And Sereny concludes her book with these words: 'No child in prostitution wants to be a prostitute. They long to be wanted—as children. They long to be loved. They long to be children'. If the practitioners are willing to stay with these young people and work through the pain in their lives by listening carefully and asking the right questions, then young people in prostitution can be led forward to regain some of that lost childhood and innocence. It is possible, as McMullan says, if we believe in 'human inherent goodness'.

Part three

11   The future

'Sleeping out is people's way of telling society that they don't want to come back into it. Being out on the pavement is a statement in itself.' (Alan Franks, *Down and Out of Sight, The Times.*)

'Homelessness in London has been a problem of growing dimensions and intractability since 1947. The upward trend in numbers has rarely been interrupted in the past forty years.' (John Greve, *Investigation into Homelessness in London, Interim Report 1985.*)

The homeless community
No one working in this field foresees any dramatic change in the situation. Youth homelessness is a growing problem and there are no indications that this trend is likely to be reversed. On the other hand, no one foresees a dramatic upsurge either.

The trend of young people coming into Central London has not been reversed over the past two decades, but workers feel some brake needs to be put on it if the whole system is not to clog up. While migration down from Scotland, the North and the Midlands continues, the drift of the homeless is now as much, if not more, from London itself, the Home Counties and the South East. For this reason it is felt that future development ought to take place not in the centre of London but in individual boroughs, to stem the flow from those areas. With the gentrification of the Soho area, there is some feeling that the centre might expand more out towards Earls Court in one direction and Kings Cross in the other. However, no one feels that young people will stop coming into the heart of London. They'll come simply because it is the centre, but they may well move out more quickly if more emergency provision is located outside the area.

The homeless population will become younger, if the indications of the past couple of years are anything to go by. Workers see additional problems arising not just because of age, but because of the unrealistic way in which younger people approach independence.

The type of young person becoming homeless is also changing. Those with jobs and skills are becoming more evident as are those

who want to continue with 'A' levels or to go on to Further
Education. There is some concern as to how these young people
can both be supported financially and found accommodation that
will be suited to the pursuit of those studies.

Unemployment
Despite the fall in unemployment, workers feel that it will still
have a major influence on families for a long time to come and
that young people will continue to be forced out of home as a
direct result. There are also concerns that the Youth Training
Scheme courses are being presented to the young as the only way
of obtaining benefit, without any attempt to see what courses will
meet their needs and aspirations. It is also felt that not enough
is being done by agencies to help young people to find work and
that staff are underestimating the level of difficulty a young person
has in staying in employment.

The changing benefit system
No one sees DHSS offices improving or becoming better staffed.
The fear of most workers that the changes in the system of claiming
benefit from April 1988 will make things harder for the young
seems to have been realised. The new benefit arrangements, with
rates related to age and not perceived need, have made it probable
that many young people will either have to remain at home
'trapped in their bedrooms', or find ways around this new
legislation. Many workers fear that the young will try to survive
without claiming benefit with a consequent growth in stealing,
begging and other DHSS-related crimes.

By introducing new board-and-lodging restrictions, the
government believes it will bring charges for board and lodging
down to a realistic level and will ensure that many young people,
who in their judgement ought to have remained with their families
until they had attained true economic independence, will return
home. However, this ignores the reasons why so many have had
to leave home in the first place and will serve only to add to the
dilemma of any young person having to move out.

Certainly the changes in the benefit system have highlighted
this dilemma. The revised income support levels have left young
people in board and lodging with very little money of their own.
Further changes will exacerbate this trend. The government aims
to make the DHSS no longer responsible for the housing costs

of the young unemployed in board and lodging. Instead the young will receive their income support entitlement with housing costs covered by housing benefit. However, the latter will not exclude the young from paying water rates and twenty per cent of domestic rates if both form part of the board-and-lodging charge. Housing benefit will also not involve rebates for fuel costs and any meals provided. Consequently, the young will have to make up the difference between what housing benefit will pay and what the board-and-lodging charge actually is. The Policy Studies Institute has estimated that, after deductions, those under the age of twenty-five, living in bed and breakfast may well be left with as little as £2.00 spending money a day to cover essentials such as meals other than breakfast, clothing, laundry and transport costs incurred in the search for work.

However, the April 1988 changes have had a more immediate impact on the young homeless. Income support is now paid in arrears and the young now have to wait two weeks before receiving benefit. This has had the effect of excluding bed and breakfast as an option for the young homeless. Hoteliers require money up front. The bed-and-breakfast places used by the young are not the type that allow for payment at the end of the stay. In fact it is not uncommon for the young to lose their accommodation because their weekly allowance has arrived a day late.

Emergency shelters are also feeling the effects of the changes. Centrepoint has noted a thirty-five per cent rise in numbers using its provision in 1988. What is of greater significance, however, is the effect the changes have had on the ability of projects to move the young homeless on from such emergency shelter. Payment in arrears means that the young have to stay longer in such shelters because they lack the means to move out. However, the pressure of larger numbers of young homeless wanting to move in has meant that other young people have had to be put out back on to the streets to make way for them.

The changes in the way the Social Fund is now administered make it that much harder to house the young. For those agencies that offer resettlement programmes, their ability to help the young set up home is greatly restricted and is likely to remain so. They point to proposed changes in a new Housing Bill that will give little incentive to landlords to let property except at the highest price they can obtain. Indeed many workers argue that the April 1988 changes are a radical departure from the way in which we operate the safety net for the poorest members of society.

Essentially, young, single people are the lowest priority. The majority of payments from the Social Fund will clearly be loans rather than grants and the Social Fund manual makes it clear that young, healthy people will not be classed as high priority for such loans. Indeed, Central London DHSS management has already stated that the young, healthy homeless in London will be 'extremely unlikely' to be given a crisis loan if in need.

This shift from a system that balances discretion and entitlement to one that is solely discretionary leaves the young homeless without clear guidance as to what they might be given and workers unsure as to the best advice they can offer. Many feel that with the withdrawal of an independent appeals system, welfare rights no longer exist. Some workers have stated that their attempts to help young people cope is bringing them into direct conflict with authority and they clearly have misgivings about the stance they have been forced to take. They do not want to encourage the young to break the law, yet they feel they have at least to turn a blind eye to some minor transgressions, for example, where work is undertaken on a temporary, part-time basis, cash in hand, to supplement income. Workers feel that this emphasis on loans rather than grants is bound to continue to create many problems and they argue that the most predictable outcome of it all will be a worrying increase in debt.

There are indications that some young people are already struggling. The scale of the changes in April 1988 placed local authorities under great pressure and computerised systems have taken time to adjust. As a consequence the effects of the changes have taken time to filter through the system and some young people in hostels were ignorant as to what these changes really implied. They are now being faced with demands for repayment of excess benefit since April. In addition, there are delays in the processing of Social Fund loans and some projects have been forced to serve notices to quit on some of their residents to speed up responses from the DHSS.

Those young people who do obtain somewhere to live are now faced with finding the extra money to pay for the cost of heating, lighting and cooking. The withdrawal of furniture grants is a particular hardship and can make the difference between survival and being forced out on to the streets. Many young people are in genuine need and their level of income makes it an impossible task for them to' pay off in eighteen months any loan that might be given. It is no wonder that workers feel that many young people will be increasingly drawn into a life of begging, stealing and prostitution to survive.

There is no doubt that, faced with existing difficulties, some young people are returning home. It is clear that some DHSS offices are assisting those who have come to London from afar to make that return possible. However, many of those who choose to return do so in the knowledge that what they can expect from home is at best neglect and at worst physical and emotional punishment. There is some evidence to suggest that agencies are beginning to meet a more desperate and frustrated group of young people. They see little point in trying to cope with the system and their bitterness, anger and dejection is too often spilling over into a verbal and physical abuse of those trying to help them.

The story of *John*, aged nineteen, is just one example. He arrived in London in the summer of 1987 penniless and needing support. Initially, he was put up at an emergency hostel and helped to apply for benefit. However, two weeks after applying, he admitted to giving false information and a fresh application had to be made. A few days later he returned to the advice centre feeling very low and wanting to talk about past experiences of being a victim of sexual assaults in a park near his home. His parents were divorced and his mother had washed her hands of him.

He was placed in a medium-stay hostel but was asked to leave after a few days because he had abused the rules. He lost his possessions and his identification documents. He mixed with some young people who had a very detrimental influence on him and he briefly entered the world of drugs. He has returned to the advice centre continuously throughout 1988 seeking support.

John wanted to enter a therapeutic community which he felt would offer him the best environment to help him come to terms with the difficulties in his life, exacerbated by his homelessness and unsettled lifestyle. Eventually, he could stand his situation no longer and decided to return home. His mother again refused to help and his father, while promising to send money for the journey home, showed little love or consideration for him. John admitted that his father would probably act violently towards him on his return and would offer him little security or hope for the future.

Workers trying to help this young person feel a deep sense of frustration at his plight despite all their attempts to help him. They describe John as a nineteen-year-old child, lost in society and in his own inner hell of suppressed, horrifying experiences of being exploited by adults.

The changes in the benefit system make life more difficult for the young homeless and they make young people like John that more vulnerable to the debilitating effects of homelessness.

From September 1988 the general entitlement to income support will be taken away from young people under eighteen years of age who have left school. They will be expected to register at a careers office, at a job centre or for a place on the YTS scheme. Regulations will allow for the payment of income support for a limited period while a job or a YTS place is obtained. However, when this period elapses, no benefits will be paid to those who have failed to secure either employment or a place on a training scheme. The proposals do allow for exceptions, but it is clear that the vast majority of the young homeless will not fall into that category.

Workers are very concerned at these changes. The proposal to link benefit to training schemes ignores completely the difficulties that homeless young people have in trying to find somewhere to live. Without a secure base it is clear that many young people will not survive such schemes. Little thought has been given as to what happens to those young people who, for a whole variety of reasons, will either be unable to cope or will need substantial support to complete their training successfully. In 1987 almost 9,000 young people had not been found a place on a YTS scheme by Christmas. In 1988, because the scheme has been extended to cover both sixteen and seventeen-year-old school leavers, the numbers are likely to be higher. This does not bode well for the young homeless in London who are, of necessity, far more vulnerable than their peers who stay at home and are therefore less likely to maintain a place on the scheme.

The whole thrust of the new benefit changes is to keep young people at home. Ironically, their effect may well be to increase the numbers of those leaving home who are forced to seek help from agencies in London. It is also possible that they may well bring closer a situation as in some American cities, where gangs of young people will exist outside of the law and outside of those agencies who give support. Without accommodation, without money or employment, these young people will have nothing to look forward to and the fear is that they will become easy prey for those whose aim is to disrupt and destroy the existing social fabric. The homeless young person can all too easily become a willing source of cannon fodder for such a cause.

Political pressures
The proposed community charge or poll tax, it is felt, will accelerate the move away from home. Young people whose homes are already overcrowded or who have little income will find the pressures overwhelming and there is no doubt that this aspect of the proposed legislation is a cause of great concern, despite the provisos it contains.

The debilitating tension between central and local government will continue. Rate capping, especially in London boroughs, will continue to affect the poor and the vulnerable and will affect the provision available for all homeless. The young are very much at the bottom of that heap and workers do not see any hope for improvement.

Increasingly, the continual reinterpretation of vulnerability by local councils of the 1977 Act will force more young people on to the streets as being ineligible for housing. The restraints placed on local authorities in refurbishing existing stock and creating new building, while at the same time encouraging the sale of council housing, has led them to accuse the government of adding to their burdens while reducing their ability to cope with them. This is part of the continual clash between Left and Right and between local and central control of services. It plays politics with the needs of the homeless and with those of the young in particular.

The housing crisis
It is hard to put into words the despair felt about the trend in housing. Words like crisis, chaos and total collapse are commonly used to explain the way in which people see the future. The perception that government is not willing to spend money and that the single homeless are not seen as priority leads workers to conclude that the situation can only remain bleak for some time to come. Some feel that unless steps are taken to remedy the problem, London will have the worst housing crisis outside the Third World.

Many other aspects arising out of the scarcity of accommodation are having and will continue to have serious repercussions on the young homeless. The growing insistence on local-borough connections leaves the homeless from outside London in limbo. The rise in rents, the practice of some landlords of squeezing the maximum out of the DHSS and the refusal to rent to those on the dole will decrease the number of places for the young even further.

Families are becoming smaller and there is more demand for those smaller units of accommodation that the single homeless require. The proposed selling off of estates to housing associations and private landlords will take a lot of short-life housing out of the market as will the pressure on councils to sell off empty property. The trend in some places to offer contracts with only short-term security, based on ability to pay, is placing pressure higher up the market that will affect availability of move-on places for the young lower down. The option for the young to squat or sleep rough is fast becoming their only option and many forecast an increase in number of those living on the street, disowning the whole accommodation system.

Coupled with all this is the desire among the young not to live in traditional-type hostels because of their rules and the lack of privacy and independence in them. More young people are opting for shared or self-contained units that are small and secure. For those needing support this has implications for staffing requirements. In general the current provision of hostel accommodation is required, but more independent options are needed if staff are not to be stuck with depressed young people feeling trapped in short-term accommodation.

Many young people will turn to squatting because they are dissatisfied with the accommodation available to the single homeless and because they are unable to afford either the rents or the down payment now required in many rented properties. Many do not know their rights and are often easily put off by a refusal from landlords, even where social security have pledged both the down payment and the rent.

There is growing concern at the numbers of young people who are found sleeping out all over London and not just in the traditional centres. Workers point to an increase over the past four years that shows no signs of diminishing. It is very easy for young people to be caught up in this lifestyle and many do not go to agencies simply because they do not know them or just do not think about the sort of support they might get from them.

The demand for services

It is felt that fewer young people from all backgrounds will choose to use existing provision in the future. No one can obviously put figures on this, but there is a growing feeling that what is being offered is demeaning and just not related to need. It is also felt that the numbers of those who once used the provision and now do not will also grow, because the attitudes and lifestyles of these young people will increasingly not fit into the mainstream of provision that seems to be going more and more 'up market'.

The demand for particular services will grow. Workers feel that the need for work with young women will grow because they will become more vulnerable in society. No decline in drug problems among young people is forecast, primarily because there isn't the money to respond to the need. Likewise, alcohol will continue to be a serious aspect of some youth homelessness. Services here are limited not just because of money but because of the general conception that the young and alcohol are not viewed as a cause for concern. Yet they are and workers feel little will be done as long as drugs are the main focus of attention.

The growth of the number of mentally ill young people is a particular worry for the future. The burden of living on their own in hard-to-let, high-rise flats on rough, run-down estates is already proving too great. West End agencies cannot provide the specialist help needed and there is great concern about how those young, needy, hard-to-satisfy, hard-to-reach youngsters, whose require- ments are manifold, are to be helped.

Young people and prostitution

The young may turn more to a life of prostitution as a way of financing their homelessness, though again there are no hard facts to back this up, but rather a feeling that is based on the trend among the young over the past few years. This is a complex issue made more difficult by its hidden and secret lifestyles and the general lack of understanding among workers of the issues involved.

However, no one is in any doubt that work for this group of young people is essential. The rent-boy scene, especially, is seen as the greatest growth area and the need to help these young boys coupled with the dangers they now face from Aids and Aids- related illnesses, is a concern that is being very widely expressed. Aids will also affect drug users more. As money becomes harder to obtain, the temptation to go into prostitution to finance a drug habit will grow, along with the exposure to risk of contamination. The need to look at this issue now and prepare for the consequences of Aids among young people is seen as a priority by all agencies.

Ethnic groups

Most of the problems faced by Black groups are not likely to be resolved quickly, as has already been made clear. However, there are immediate concerns about how to cope with the growing lack of motivation among some Black youngsters to help themselves and their lack of care and security in their own homes.

On the other hand, many young Black people are increasingly not prepared to accept second best. They want to own their own houses and they value much more now their own privacy and independence. There is concern that the next five years might be very crucial in Black/White relationships. Until young Black people feel they have a stake in the community, they will not support those forces who uphold law and order. They see it as futile to defend that which is not theirs and see no wrong in destroying and pulling down.

As the adult Caribbean population becomes older and dies off, there is some concern for the future. There is a fear that the next decade will see a very different English Black of Afro-Caribbean origin, someone very dangerous to deal with because he or she will lack the sympathy and understanding of today's Black adults. The lid is only just being kept on at present. As the young Black comes into his or her own, there is a great danger that many will upset, overthrow and destroy the present order to gain justice.

Young people from care

The growth in the number of homeless youngsters from local authority care is an issue that many workers want to see tackled. There is an appeal to all those working with the young in care not to draw a distinction between the leaving-care and the leaving-home population. The issues are the same and in both cases there is little done to help the young make a successful transition. So many care situations give no or inadequate preparation for the move. Local authorities have to be pushed to work closely with social services, housing and voluntary groups if some of the injustices to the leaving-care population are to be remedied. The notion that a young person in care is ready for independence just because a certain chronological age is reached has no basis in good child care. The trend of literally paying off difficult youngsters because they are too difficult to manage has to be reversed.

The nature of the care offered to young people has also to be examined and re-evaluated if the bitterness of those in care is to be addressed. So many who come on to the homeless circuit are resentful, escaping from a system which they feel does them little good. Efforts must be made to link up good housing availability with leaving care and the trend has to be away from the idea that the quality of support depends on where you live in relation to your previous home in care. Flexibility of support over long periods is essential regardless of where an individual lives or what type of provision he or she lives in. Young people in and just out of care deserve far more than they are receiving or perceive themselves to receive. Those on the homeless circuit will only begin to be reduced when support systems are designed that stick with youngsters and not to them and are flexible to be adjusted to individual need. To do this the trend has to be to bring the providers and the young together, to promote more in-service planning and the setting out of policy so that young people can have a forum where they will be listened to.

Conclusion
It is clear, therefore, that the problem of the young single homeless is not going to disappear. The concern is that the new benefit system and new legislation such as the community charge will make the situation worse, while at the same time the ability of local authorities and voluntary organisations to offer support to the young homeless will be undermined.

12 Towards a consensus

'Many in Britain still think our housing crisis only affects a
few. How can we compare ourselves to the problems of
drought-stricken Africa? The answer is that we don't. We
compare the extremes of wealth and poverty in our own
society. It is no great comfort to the person sleeping rough
in London to think that there is someone worse off somewhere else.' (Sheila McKechnie, *Shelter Progress Report 1987.*)

The future – which direction?

It is clear from earlier chapters that a great deal is already being
undertaken in Central London, especially by voluntary agencies,
to give the young single homeless the support their predicament
demands. Many are working very hard, often under severe physical and financial constraints. The work carried out by these
agencies ought not to be underestimated. While much of this
report reflects in many ways the agencies' own criticisms of
themselves and their work, it is also a testimony to the level of
individual endeavours and commitment to the young in need that
has been maintained for more than a decade with little official
recognition of its value.

The agencies, on the other hand, would be the first to admit
the limitations and deficiencies of the services they are able to offer,
reaching only a small proportion of those in need and incapable
of tackling the roots of the problems of this group. With the trends
discussed in the previous chapter, the inadequacy of current
provision becomes an even greater cause of concern.

The problems facing the young who are homeless and at risk
are diffuse and complex. It is not an area of work where there
are simple solutions. It attracts many theories and philosophies
about what are the right or wrong ways of helping such young
people. The agencies talked to in the course of this investigation
have been remarkably open about their needs and priorities. There
is no consensus of opinion, however, as to what should be done
next and in some ways the agencies are looking for clarification
and direction about the way forward.

The question is how to develop a coherent local and national
policy to support the young homeless. Five components have

stood out in all the discussions held with those working with the young homeless.

Reliable information is essential, especially sound statistical information that can bring home to the public the extent of the problem. Linked to that is the need for *social and political education,* for the problem cannot be tackled effectively unless it is seen as a pressing national issue. In this context many have argued for the creation of a Ministry of Youth to co-ordinate policy and provision for the young across a number of ministries. At another level, agencies, voluntary and statutory, should collaborate, formally and informally, to provide *a coherent and integrated service.* Much more *counselling advice and support* ought to be available for young people, especially in the local area at the point when they make the decisions to move away from home. There are some splendid, but isolated, exceptions to this, but largely the young have no one to turn to, and there is an argument that says some would not leave home altogether if advocacy was readily available. Most of all there must be *housing provision,* especially in London boroughs. This alone, if readily available, would alleviate some of the worst consequences of homelessness in society. This then might avoid the type of comment quoted by Waters (1982) from a CHAR report: 'We want to say that a lot of the problems of hostels are caused because they are hostels. . . . What you have done is to turn us into hostel dwellers and force us to adopt a way of life you disapprove of'.

The need for research

The lack of consensus as to what is necessary for these young people has, at least partly, to do with a lack of knowledge in the agencies about the young people themselves: who they are, what their needs are and how they see their needs being met. There is very little research carried out in this area of work and with it very little evaluation of the efficacy and relevance of what is offered. This is largely due to lack of finances and the inability of staff to have time to follow up the work they do. This is not to discredit individual pieces of research that are produced by projects and which help to keep the issue of these young people alive. It is accepted, however, that a lack of serious, in-depth research is detrimental both to practice and to the ability of the general public and government to understand the issues involved. Because of this, the tabloid image of the young homeless predominates, eliciting little sympathy apart from twinges of conscience at Christmas time.

There is a clear requirement that any piece of work set up in London must be constituted as a piece of action research. The research has to be built into the daily structures so that there can be a better understanding of the type of young people who enter the agencies and the reasons why their lives have taken particular directions. It can also offer young people a better opportunity to understand themselves and make sense of the issues that surround their leaving home.

Many workers have argued that research must begin with outreach work that targets those on the margins, untouched by existing provision and largely abandoned. This would include those sleeping rough or in squats, young boys on the rent scene, young females into prostitution and those young people with drug difficulties.

Research that could be co-ordinated to offer a comprehensive review of the extent, difficulties and requirements of homeless Black youngsters is a major and pressing requirement. This is one aspect of the approach necessary to avoid the differential treatment of ethnic minorities who are most at risk of disadvantage. There is little understanding of this area of work among many existing agencies and much less in the corridors of power in local and national government.

Because issues are complex, however, they will not be clarified by a single piece of research. Ideally, individual pieces of inquiry should link up with work carried out by other agencies to give a co-ordinated picture. Ultimately, this research should have a twofold aim. It should inform those working in the field of the issues involved and directly help to influence practice and training. In addition, it should be the basis on which agencies can inform public opinion and campaign in government circles to win the resources that these young people need.

It is generally accepted that no accurate way has yet been found to quantify young homelessness and there is a clear need for national statistics. In particular, there is a growing demand to find a way of measuring the numbers of children and juveniles that go missing from home each year. Although the police do document the numbers of missing persons, only eight of fifty-two areas record the numbers of those under seventeen years of age. There is no way of knowing how many young people run away, how often they do so, where they run to, or what happens to them. Without this information there is little chance that a national co-ordinated forum to identify needs and implement reforms can be effectively set up. The Children's Society has pioneered work with young runaways and would welcome any research provision that would help them co-ordinate the task they are doing so that a comprehensive national picture can emerge. It is a difficult task and is by rights a national responsibility, but some workers feel that if the task could be begun in London, it would help co-ordinate and develop services for these young people.

None of this can be brought about unless some way is found to impart the correct information on a continuous basis to those who have the ability to alter existing statutes and policies. The literature on this matter calls continually for on-going monitoring rather than regular surveys. It stresses that local authorities should have this built into their structures so that relevant provision can be set up to alleviate local homelessness and help avoid the frightening, intimidating and dangerous harassment to which so many young people are subject.

The way forward

With a co-ordinated research programme underway, society must then mount a two-pronged attack on the problem of the young homeless: first by taking steps to reduce the number of people in this unfortunate predicament and then by improving the support available to those young people for whom homelessness is the only option.

The arrival of Dr Barnardo's, and any other major charity, on this scene will be welcomed, not because they can suddenly wave magic wands and turn all the Cinderellas into princesses. Such an approach would be greatly resented and resisted, for agencies are rightly proud of what has been built up. Rather, there is a need to recognise that existing work can be supported by helping to assist and improve the quality of resources already present. Any agency that is willing to co-operate with present provision and can tactfully and sensitively develop policy and practice will receive a great deal of goodwill and support.

Susanna Agnelli (1986) points out in her book that the Chinese expression for the word 'crisis' consists of two characters: one that signifies 'problem', the other 'opportunity'. What she is emphasising is that in all the gloom surrounding the plight of the young who are homeless and at risk and the lack of response from those in authority, there can be a lot of scope for initiative and positive action. There is no doubt that this is so in London. Part of the approach needed is to see the young for what they are, as people of intrinsic worth, and not what they have become through circumstances. As Agnelli points out, part of the tragedy of these young people may be that they are far less attractive as objects of compassion than many others. Their needs and the plight of homelessness too often take second place to the sensationalism that emphasises the dropout, the drug addict, the dosser and the prostitute. Justice and compassion demands that this distortion be countered and every effort made to give our young a future.

13 Reducing the problem

'Being homeless is one possible consequence of trying to change homes and establish independence. Youth is a time for exploring and taking risks before settling down. Many homeless show considerable courage and resourcefulness in contrast to the sickly and helpless portraits frequently sketched by the project reports. In other settings these young people would have merited the Duke of Edinburgh's gold award or achieved a single-handed Atlantic crossing. The "technological", hard, practical approach of services denies the imagination, adventure and meaning in people's lives. These efforts deserve respect.' (David Brandon *et al, The Survivors. A Study of Homeless Young Newcomers to London and the Responses Made to Them.*)

It is the opinion of all those working with the young single homeless in London that only a small proportion of this group actually make use of the available services. Until the research described in Chapter 12 is complete, there will be no accurate picture of the true size of the problem.

This much is clear, however. The problem is a serious one, there are no indications that it is decreasing and action must be taken now if trends are to be reversed and if the problem is not to get out of control.

Raising the profile
Research is only one aspect of a wider educational process which agencies feel is essential if their work is to progress.

Much more needs to be carried out in schools so that leaving home becomes an integral part of the curriculum and is not just something that is added on to programmes in the final term. Before that can happen, there must be an attempt to put across the argument that the expectations and aspirations of young people about leaving home are valid and reasonable, and that it is part of the transition from adolescence to adulthood, with a context around housing, homelessness and the wish of young people to progress.

In particular, the young themselves need to know clearly the realities involved and the difficulties that they will have to overcome. So many workers have commented on the ignorance of those coming into London with regard to the availability of jobs and the cost of housing. Even Londoners face the same charge and few are aware of what they can do or what is theirs by right. That is why many have argued that one of the major obstacles to their work is the lack of local provision that could give young people advice, support and practical help and so prevent many making the trek to London and into the centre of London in particular. Unless efforts can be made to stem the tide of young people that do come in, it is felt that less will be available for them simply because resources are scarce and becoming harder to find.

At present, doing something positive in this area is interpreted as encouraging the young to leave home. Yet unless this issue is allowed a public hearing, its resolution will still be prey to the charge of being bitty and ineffective. The process begins by winning the argument nationally and in government about the right of young people to leave home. This then demands that local provision and support offset detrimental images of homelessness allowing young people to see their experiences in a context and to make informed choices.

Thus the need to awaken individual and community consciences to the needs of the young single homeless is one of the major hurdles to be overcome. Too often attempts at public education are limited to dramatic and sensational accounts of cardboard cities and park bench living, particularly at Christmas or in times of extreme cold. As Waters (1982) points out, such attempts may produce donations but they also have the effect of further alienating the single homeless 'by perpetuating cultural stereotypes'. That is why in 1987 the National Council of Voluntary Organisations called for lessons on leaving home to be part of the curriculum. In this way leaving home would be placed in a context and preventative work could be begun with those who felt the need to move away.

Greve and his team (1986) recommended that a standing conference on homelessness be set up so that all the activities carried out on behalf of the homeless in London could be facilitated and co-ordinated. In addition, their earlier report (1985) recommended that a whole series of policies which affected homelessness should be reviewed and monitored. Among these were the revised board and lodging payments; the implementation of the care in the community policy; the closures of hostels and resettlement units; the disjunction between capital and revenue funding; the operation of the Homeless Persons Act; and the General Needs Index.

The plight of the young homeless in London is largely unknown and the young themselves lack an effective champion of their cause. Workers in London have welcomed the growing interest of the major charities in this area of work and have been excited about the possibilities that their intervention might have. Many workers have pressed that Dr Barnardo's use its position as a major charity to assist the campaign to raise the issues about these young people with those who have the power to make changes. They feel that such an approach which outlined the aspirations of the young to have somewhere to live and the wherewithal to pay for it could be very effective. This support would not be an encouragement to young people to leave home, but it would challenge the assertion that the best place for all young people is at home.

The major charities are urged to combine to present an effective lobby in Parliament on the issues. It is felt that those who run these charities have experience in dealing with those who are in government and can influence the direction of policy. Such a lobby on a concerted basis might be hard to ignore. The agencies in London argue that they have neither the experience nor the clout to make an effective impact.

Improving the housing provision

A homeless young person needs somewhere to live above all else. This goes without saying. Everyone has a right to somewhere that is safe and secure and can be called home. Without this basic necessity it is asking too much of the young to make a success of the other practical and emotional issues in their lives.

The lack of suitable accommodation for all levels of young people is the biggest obstacle agencies have to face. The system is so clogged up that spaces are at a premium. Youngsters have to be moved on or out as the case may be, so that others can have the opportunity to cope.

CHAR, the Campaign for the Homeless and Rootless, insists that accommodation must be funded and managed by local housing authorities as an integral part of their service, for only local authorities have the resources to manage housing to acceptable standards. Even where voluntary bodies can provide good provision, CHAR argues that they do not have satisfactory access to housing resources to meet their users' long-term needs. The cuts in local authority budgets underline this. Short-life property groups have suffered from the lack of revenue funding to make

empty property habitable. Councils are likewise not releasing property that may be part of a future funding programme, even though it may have to stand empty for some time and the short-life group has the finance and the manpower to effect renovation.

The principal need in all this is one of individual autonomy and for the provision of such housing that enhances people's control over their own lives. For the young it demands an increase in single-person accommodation as the only realistic way of dealing effectively with present homelessness and preventing it in the future.

David Brandon (1980) was clear that projects for the homeless must also have the facility to refer outwards to rented accommo-dation or squats, to prevent the young from being involved in what he termed the incestuous process of being referred further along the homeless circuit and going through a miserable personal crisis before being housed. The problem is, as Greve pointed out in his 1985 report, revenue funding bodies concentrate on short-stay accommodation, and the medium-care and longer-stay, perma-nent, supported and unsupported, accommodation, which is desperately needed, is the most difficult type of provision to fund. There is a consensus of opinion that these fundamental issues will only be resolved if attempts are made in government to plan the number of houses to be built or renovated, to set targets for such housing and achieve them, to recognise the beneficial and economic effects of housing and to get methods of financing housing right.

There is consensus too that the young want permanent and self-contained accommodation. A DHSS report in 1976 supported this view by stating that sufficient accommodation should be available so that any young person who wished to live independently could do so. Madeline Drake et al (1982) found that many youngsters wanted their own bedroom in a shared flat, house or small hotel, and a number were quite prepared to share amenities. Others argue for hostels that allow for privacy, give security of tenure, that can be used as employment addresses and allow the young to come and go outside fixed hours.

Thus an article in 1985 (Holmes 1985) suggested that the govern-ment should consider building halls of residence for up to one hundred young people who were not considering further or higher education. The idea was that if such halls were opened in large cities and towns which had a substantial population of young claimants and young homeless, it could ease some of the housing crisis. A similar idea is suggested by Julia Unwin, the co-ordinator of the WECVS, with the aim of allowing young people to look after themselves with a minimal amount of structure and support.

Those in greatest need fall between the ages of fifteen-and-a-half and nineteen, with particular emphasis on the sixteen- to seventeen-year-olds. Accommodation is needed that will allow these young people to make the transition from adolescence to adulthood in safety and security. Agencies are clear that accommodation that has structure and support is necessary for this group. It is generally accepted that putting a roof over someone's head is only the first step. It is not enough to place youngsters in such a setting and then step back and let them get on with their lives. It is also a clear requirement, however, that structures should be flexible and allow the individual to make mistakes, while receiving support and stimulation at a distance. For some young people that support will have to be on the premises, twenty-four hours a day. For others, it will need to be near enough to call on, yet far enough away not to intrude. The emphasis has to be on young people opting into support rather than having it placed upon them.

The nature of this support will vary. Help and assistance for young people at different stages of their emotional and independent development that is more than just sensitive housing management is essential. Drake (1982) said that one-third of her sample needed supportive regimes. Most of this group she felt could cope with minimal peripatetic support in totally unstaffed accommodation, but some needed a warden and part-time residential help, while a small minority required a fully staffed hostel. NACRO (1981) agreed with that balance of provision, but also argued for lodging houses and landlady-type provision within families.

Advice, assessment and counselling should also be available for the young and practical help with work and education is an option that some would like to have included. Workers have stressed that the young need rules and regulations in their accommodation if they are to have a chance to succeed, but they stress that there must be a balance between what is essential for good order, especially in communal living, and what will allow the individual privacy and freedom of action.

There is some consensus that more accommodation ought to be provided for young women so that they can determine their futures without the stresses that sharing with males can bring. Some of the hidden homelessness among women is attributed to mixed-sexed hostels, which in practice often mean male-dominated hostels, and the lack of single-sexed provision. Some of this accommodation needs to be safe and secure, staffed only by females, and offering support to a variety of need. An element of this need that is not catered for is provision for young women who are pregnant that would allow security and support during and after pregnancy with access to move-on accommodation. It is recognised that this is not an easy option to provide, but its glaring lack is one that ought to be remedied.

Lack of move-on accommodation causes the greatest frustration among workers and the young alike. Projects argue that a through-flow system is essential, but shortage of finances and available property, in addition to local authority practices, mean that the young are too often stuck in medium-term accommodation, unable to move out.

The consequence is that the young are imprisoned in whatever housing is provided for them. Only through the integration of all services, statutory and voluntary, can this situation begin to be remedied. Andrew Purkis (1982) would add that services should not only be applied accurately to individual need, but should be done in a way that is of interest to the users themselves and to society at large. Too many resources, he feels, are wasted on standardised and inaccurate solutions.

The type of accommodation is also important. Many workers feel that old-style hostels are disliked by the young because they are seen to be rigid and impersonal. More small living units that allow privacy yet allow for communal living, where young people can be in touch with both those of their own age and adults, are required. Most of all accommodation has to be reasonably and realistically priced so as not to deter those who have just begun working and not overburden those who want to pursue further education.

In the meantime, many young people will live in hostels for varying lengths of time. London has lost a great deal of bed space in these last few years when demand has been rising, as Greve (1985) points out. Those that are left can be open to criticism in the way they are managed. It is distressing to see hostels which seem to be run on the proviso that anything will do for the young. A well-run hostel ought to have good standards of hygiene and cleanliness, good facilities, and single rooms for privacy, and allow for elements of independence regarding the provision of keys, self-catering and social facilities.

However, in common with the wishes of young people, all workers have stressed their opposition to the creation of ghettos for the young homeless that prevent them from playing their full part in the community. CHAR (1985) speaks for many when it says that the young must not be relegated to areas of 'urban and industrial blight'. Provision has to be set up within easy access of a local urban area, close to public transport and community services to prevent the young homeless from being isolated from the community. Andrew Purkis argues that housing is not an end in itself, but, as someone's home, is a means to life as a member of society. Home is the individual's 'emotional and psychological centre', and if the location of that provision prevents someone working, shopping, or maintaining a social life, then it is not meeting some of the most important needs of the individual.

Changing the law and official policies
For the needs of the young homeless to be met, they first have to be recognised. The latest white paper on housing, however, does not mention homelessness or the homeless. There are no proposals to help the homeless or deal with the increasingly poor state of the housing stock.

It is accepted that the 1977 Homeless Persons Act was a break-through and there is no doubt that many have benefited from it. However, Hilditch (1982) puts into words the opinions of many when he asserts that the Act has been undermined and is not being operated compassionately because, in general, the homeless are blamed and stigmatised and are often the recipients of degrading treatment. He feels, as many do, that abuses of the Act, particularly by the young, are minimal and do not warrant the 'Costa del Dole'-type headlines. The failure lies in the lack of statutory force given to the Act's Code of Guidance that leads to distinctions between the 'deserving' and 'undeserving' and turns away the very people the Act is designed to help.

A homeless person, or a person threatened by homelessness, ought to be able to apply to any housing authority for help with accommodation. As homelessness is too often a crisis matter, there is the assumption that councils would offer some form of twenty-four-hour service or at least be open to all callers during working hours. However, in recent years local authorities in London have been closing homeless persons units for long periods and accepting applications, if any, only on the telephone. Lambeth and Brent have had units closed for long periods for some time. Camden, with one of the largest homeless populations, has now shut down its unit. This is a clear sign of the level of breakdown in provision of services for those homeless who are termed as a priority. It is clear that the outlook for the non-priority young is bleak.

This is why so many workers argue that both the 1977 and the 1985 Housing Acts should be amended so that they become a safety net for all the homeless, especially the young. There is a clear body of opinion that wants to see sixteen- to eighteen-year-olds treated as a priority because of their vulnerability at that age. Sixteen-year-olds should be placed on waiting lists so that their needs can be carefully considered, and workers feel that local councils must be made legally responsible for housing them.

Workers argue that the single homeless should be allowed to register on waiting lists while still in hostels, bed and breakfast and lodgings and be eligible to gain points on an amended scheme so that they can be given accommodation within a reasonable time scale. There should also be a choice as to the area and type of accommodation they prefer so that their needs, especially if they are in employment, can be catered for.

NACRO (1981) called for a definition of homelessness that would also include those living in situations with no security of tenure and at risk of being forced to seek alternative accommodation within a time period which they consider to be immediate. Among these would be included those who are due to be discharged from institutions, those living with relatives or friends in overcrowded conditions or illegal tenancies, those living in reception centres, and those living in hostels, lodging houses, cheap hotels, boarding houses, unlicensed squats and derelict buildings. In particular NACRO want 'vulnerability' to be extended to include exploitation and risk of offending, and that to be judged by those working most closely with the young people.

However, the continual re-interpretation by local councils of vulnerability in the 1977 Act is forcing more young people on to the street as being ineligible for housing.

Linked to this issue are the board and lodging regulations. In

1987 Lord Scarman attacked the slum conditions experienced by
the homeless in bed-and-breakfast hotels and equally strong con-
clusions emerged from Val Howarth's 1987 survey. The eight-week
rule in London has caused staff great difficulty in placing a young
person in long-term hostel provision. The main reason the young
do not leave home when they want to has to do with access and
resources. Staff find that many young people feel trapped at home
by these rules and often many return as the only way of getting
financial support, thus exacerbating what are already difficult
situations. These regulations are also making less space available
in bed and breakfast. It is not uncommon for young people to
sleep four to a room in such provision. Given the criticisms of
Lord Scarman and Val Howarth, it is not surprising that tensions
very soon become unbearable, especially sharing with strangers.
So, the young move on, often sleeping rough, having no patience
to wait for hostel provision to be found. Many workers feel
frustrated because often at the very moment provision is found,
the young person has disappeared.

The government makes no secret of the fact that its proposed
changes in the board and lodging regulations are aimed at keeping
expenditure under control. It argues that it will no longer allow
young people in bed and breakfast to have more spending money
than others in their age group. It believes that these regulations
will remove one deterrent to their settling down in more permanent accommodation and to taking up employment. The logic of
this is that the government remains convinced that young people
have somehow been attracted to board and lodgings by the rate
of benefit available.

This is clearly not the case and it is hard to see how these proposed regulations cannot but fail to increase the numbers of young
people homeless on London's streets. If the young homeless problem is to be reduced, it is essential that this attitude is changed
and that the new board-and-lodgings regulations be closely monitored as to their effects on the young homeless.

A consideration that cannot be ignored in any review of any
current laws and policies has to do with the work of the social
services, DHSS and housing departments. Good provision, many
feel, is directly related to the extent to which these services
co-operate with and complement each other. Too often responsibility is passed across to another department, reflecting the division in government between the Department of the Environment

and the DHSS. It is clear that the housing crisis among the young can only be eased by co-operation, in a well thought out programme, between government, local authorities and the voluntary organisations who bear so much of the brunt of the work.

Investing in ethnic minorities

Only the outlines of the difficulties facing some of the ethnic minority groups have been touched on in this report. This is a major issue in itself and is deserving of much fuller treatment. Of all the young people that have been spoken about in this book, young Black people are perhaps those with the greatest needs because of their history and their position in our society. Their isolation and the extent of their needs are not comprehended and ways have to be found to allow this section of London's community an effective voice. Moreover, both local and central government must find ways to invest in these communities and help them develop existing provision.

There is a clear need for boroughs to draw up long-term programmes, in conjunction with the voluntary sector, to identify and help eradicate policies and procedures which discriminate unfairly between groups according to race and gender. There is no doubt that young Black people are particularly vulnerable here and ways must be found for them to participate more in the community and in the making of decisions and policies.

There is no doubt that if homelessness continues at its present levels among the ethnic minorities, it will ultimately have detrimental effects on society as a whole. Homelessness has a direct link with crime, with mental illness and with poor education. Ultimately it has direct links with the security and stability of the family as the core of society. The family is destabilised by homelessness, consequently so is the community and society as a whole. Efforts must be made urgently to lift the crushing burden of homelessness off the backs of the ethnic groups, especially those of Afro-Caribbean origin and alleviate the pressure of housing on many disillusioned and largely excluded communities.

However, their needs are not confined solely to housing, though that is a pre-requisite. They are also about being valued in this society as a people of worth, as young Londoners who ought to have equal rights to education, training and employment as any other young person in the capital. The alarming increase in mental illness among young Black people as reported by workers is a clear indication of the strain in their communities. Their needs must be responded to as a matter of some urgency and responded to substantially if, as many fear, a whole generation is not to be lost to homelessness.

14 Improving the support

'The problems of relationship, efficiency and effectiveness
which have arisen can only be dealt with by close liaison,
more systematic and comprehensive joint policy making and,
in many instances, more adequate funding of voluntary
provision by local and central government.' (John Greve,
Investigation into Homelessness in London, Interim Report 1985.)

Improving funding

There is no doubt that much more needs to be done immediately
to fund projects that work with the homeless. Greve (1985)
stressed that the difficulties in obtaining revenue funding, available
often for only one year at a time, created instability in the planning
and management of these projects. Short-term, ad hoc, financial
arrangements, especially in day and evening centres, are costly,
onerous and create chronic insecurity for all concerned. Sufficient
funds must be put into local provision and there have been calls
for government to give local councils more money to spend on
renovating and building homes.

Projects in Central London have to compete for what funding
is available and cut their cloth according to what they receive.
Some staff spend time fund raising and this detracts from the level
and quality of the service offered. Such pressures mean that
projects have to spend as much time on survival as on developing
resources and meeting changing needs.

The use of volunteers is widespread and while this adds an
interesting and particular dimension to many pieces of work, there
is also a danger that such a practice can mask the quality of the
work that is being provided. There is no doubt that staff feel the
need of a great deal more impact of a professional nature, training
that would support them in the often difficult tasks they have to
undertake.

For so many the finance is not available, though many projects,
within limits, do very good work in this regard and WECVS, the
West End Co-ordinated Voluntary Service for the single homeless,
has given a great deal of support to affiliated members. However,
much more input is necessary if individual need and changing
demand are to be catered for. Some workers have argued that
funding should be co-ordinated by central government, thus

reducing the insecurity and the time wasted in the annual fight for survival. However, unless and until homelessness is recognised as a national issue, such suggestions are likely to fall on deaf ears.

Improving co-ordination

There is no doubt that the annual fight for funding does have important implications for this work. Projects are insecure and many lament the loss of the GLC because there is now no single body with the potential to co-ordinate all the work that is done for the homeless. Competition for funding has put projects into competition with each other. The result is a great deal of 'territoriality' in London agencies and at times an almost jealous desire to guard their own individual sectors.

Needless to say this does not create a climate conducive to co-ordination and togetherness, though one body, WECVS, has taken on that specific task and has clear links with a number of individual projects in Central London as well as with statutory agencies and some of the larger charities. Individual projects do have close links with each other, but in general there is little togetherness across Central London and not much sharing of ideas and practice.

Social services and probation have the closest working relationship with the voluntary sector and there is no doubt that on an individual basis a great deal of co-operation and support goes on. Overall, however, the picture is not a good one. Workers complain that these statutory services are often unreliable and inefficient, can cause more difficulties than they solve and are sometimes in as much need of support from the agencies as the young people they seek to help. The feeling is that statutory workers are under so much pressure in often disorganised departments that they are unable to receive the supervision and support necessary to carry out their roles.

Workers save their strongest criticism for the work of the DHSS offices. They are widely condemned as being unhelpful, threatening and dangerous places with little skills in handling what are often sensitive and difficult issues. Staff are said to be badly trained, inconsistent and inflexible making arbitrary decisions with no explanation to the young people involved.

Clearly, there is little hope of co-ordination in such a climate. Nonetheless, efforts have been made to co-ordinate responses to the DHSS on an individual and a group basis. The latter is co-ordinated by the Central London Social Security Advisory Forum

(CLASSAF) which assists around forty member agencies who work directly with people claiming benefit. It gives advice about claims and monitors illegalities in social security offices. On an individual basis attempts are made to have close working relationships with individual offices. This sometimes can work, but in general staff are left feeling angry and frustrated in their attempts to elicit explanations.

A few projects receive some management support from outside their agency, but in general the picture is one of a vast number of people doing a great deal of good work largely in isolation. This isolation and division is symptomatic of the approach to the homeless in government and in society at large. Effective change will only take place from the bottom up. Despite the division and territoriality that abounds in the work for the homeless, there is a great deal of energy and goodwill waiting to be tapped and channelled. This needs to be brought together and shared.

One of the criticisms of the work in London is that it is full of co-ordinators who are content only to paper over the cracks. Little is seen to be done to tackle the issues of the young homeless and to take seriously the need for re-appraisal and development. It is almost as if the work has come full circle and has returned to the point where so much of it began in the 1970s. There is a fear that so much of what is done is now irrelevant to a growing number of the young. Changes in legislation relating to homelessness present a challenge that has to be taken up. It is hardly surprising that any government has not really taken youth homelessness seriously if those working with young people have been unable to come to a consensus.

These are harsh criticisms but they reflect the impatience of so many individual workers who are asking for a constructive response. The demise of the GLC, in a non-political sense, is indicative of the move away from institutional to self-help in society. There is a gap that needs to be filled, to bring together all the work, statutory and voluntary, to share ideals and practices, to find ways of working closely together and making use of each other's skills. This is a prerequisite if change is to be effected. So far the messages are not being heard in government. Real co-ordination can change that.

Offering a flexible response

Many young people complain that they have to go through so many procedures, so much red tape, to get the service they need, that they give up. Workers have expressed their frustration at statutory and voluntary provision alike. Their feeling is that with a little more flexibility some young people in great need can be effectively helped because they have built up the courage to ask. Once that courage starts to diminish over a period of waiting, the moment is lost. It is true to say that finance governs the way in which responses can be made, but so much bureaucracy surrounds the granting of support, so many assumptions are made about what young people need that workers and young people alike become impatient and frustrated.

Much of present provision in London is office-based and fairly inflexible. Then there is the feeling that the young have that there is nowhere at present for them to come back to continuously as a base to rest and take stock of their lives. They have the feeling of always having to move on and are constrained not just by the fact of their homelessness, but are constrained by the rules and regulations of present provision that tie them down and inhibit choice. There is no permanence and stability in a life that is, of necessity, one of continual move on.

As a response to this, many workers argue that there is a need in London for a core provision around which the cluster of existing projects in any one borough can be co-ordinated and serviced. Such provision would have as its baseline a requirement to respond to the individual and not the individual to the agency. In analogous terms, it could be seen as an emergency, basic-assessment response, something like the emergency department of a busy hospital.

Such a provision would need to offer a whole range of services to the young homeless over a twenty-four-hour period and be flexible in the type of response it could make. It could offer an emergency, crash-pad facility for young people picked up on the streets by the police and needing a few hours' safety until other services are available. It could respond to requests from various authorities for support with a young person who was not necessarily in serious trouble, but who needed advice, advocacy and perhaps some counselling so that needs could be assessed. It could be the first port of call for young people coming into London for the first time and needing a base to find their feet. Some of these could be those who presently contact squatting agencies for advice and help before coming to London and who could then be passed on to existing agencies for help and support.

Some of the young people talked to saw such a provision in terms of a sanctuary for those who had to be out on the streets all day. They saw it as a place that would offer far more than just the possibility of playing pool or watching videos. They saw it being open for those times when the young homeless were most in need and mentioned especially evenings, weekends and national holidays. They obviously saw it being open during the day as well and at such times felt it could offer basic facilities for those who sleep out rough. It would be somewhere that would be open early enough for the young to wash, change, do laundry and have breakfast—all of which would set them up for the day and enable those who, for example, were going off for a job interview to be clean and smart.

The young people spoken to were very clear about who should be allowed into such a provision and what should be expected of them. It is here that the notion of 'sanctuary' is quite relevant. The young want a centre that could be free from hassle and strife. They stress the need for a place that could allow some peace in their lives, a place whose facilities would not be abused. On the other hand, rules would be at a minimum and young people would be given time and space and not feel they had to go out after a set period. This sanctuary would give them the freedom to speak to each other, to talk seriously with peers or workers, to play games or in general rest quietly from the sheer misery of being homeless.

Others felt that such a provision should offer advice about a whole range of issues relevant to the homeless. Many of these are very well covered by existing projects, but there was a request for educational facilities and practical guidance and counselling in employment matters. In particular counselling, therapy and befriending could be offered, services that could be on offer over a period of time. At present agencies are not able to offer such help in any depth and this is much regretted by workers.

Many workers see this type of provision as the central hub that could co-ordinate and unify existing work. Its essence would be to work alongside that which exists and not to overlap or duplicate. It could cross borough boundaries and link up with a variety of provision. There is an argument that says such a resource in Central London could act as a type of 'clearing house' for those from the capital and refer individuals to existing provision within their own boroughs. In this way some of the flow of young people into London could be reversed and the process of passing the young along the homeless circuit somewhat reversed.

What has been described is a complex of notions that have been expressed as priorities. Of necessity this is an idealised concept and describes what might be striven for rather than what is instantly obtainable.

A flexible-type provision of this nature could also have benefits for existing work. If it were to play a true co-ordinating role it could alleviate some of the pressures on existing work in terms of territoriality. Not only could it service existing work, but it could also help in the essential process of re-evaluation and development by monitoring need and co-ordinating research.

It is accepted that such a response would need time to evolve and be acceptable to existing provision. The proposed develop-ment at the Centre at St Martin's in the Field, due to open towards the end of 1988, is a step in the right direction. What is important is that there is a great need to find ways to respond to many youngsters who, for whatever reason, choose not to use existing provision. It is essential that structures be set up that can meet young people on their own ground, listen to their needs and try to respond accordingly.

Offering counselling and advocacy facilities
It is recognised that a clear strategy is needed to encourage adults, especially those in positions of authority, to listen to the needs of young homeless people. Agnelli (1986) points out that this is usually the first step towards the creation of a national policy. She complains that young people on the streets have too often had to make do with what she terms 'leftovers'. Advocacy she insists is complementary to provision of service and is an integral part of a wider preventative strategy.

There is certainly an argument that insists that much of what is being offered to the young homeless, especially in Central London, is incomplete and fragmented. So many young people are passed on with little questioning as to what will happen to them next. For some the teenage syndrome lasts long into their twenties as a result. A great number of workers feel strongly about this lack of an adequate counselling service for the young. They highlight the need for them to be treated as emerging adults and be given the level and quality of support they need, a support

that is tolerant and which of its essence first listens. Such counselling would be flexible, though not necessarily long term. However,
in essence it would be a service that responded to individuals,
accepted them for what they were, which would include being
sensitive to particular cultural distinctions, and would help to
connect them with themselves and their family dynamics. Workers
argue that the lack of such counselling provision is the biggest
obstacle to a young person's progress after that caused by scarcity
of accommodation.

   This counselling would also include advice about coping with
the problems of living, how to cope on their own, how to handle
debt, a hostile landlord and so on. As a practical service it would
be offered not only in the agency, but also out on the streets where
the young congregate, particularly for those who do not use
existing services. It would help the young to come to terms with
the fundamental issues about their reasons for being on the streets
and would help them to make sense of their lives in a way that
did not demand that they return continually for support.

Such services must be available not just in London. If the plight of the homeless in the capital is to be eased, then facilities must be made available in boroughs and towns all across the country. It has long been the cry of those who work with the young homeless in London that extensive services should be available at the point of leaving home, when the young person is largely free from the problems that develop from protracted homelessness.

Offering outreach work

There is no doubt that many workers lament the scarcity of outreach work. So little is known about those out on the streets, who they are and how they live, and many would agree with Saunders' assertion (1986) that outreach work is the way in which that information will be gathered. The majority of agencies are office-bound and wait for the young to come to them. As has been stated, that choice is often economical and not philosophical. However, workers argue that unless efforts are made to go out and meet the young on their own ground and attempt to respond to their needs there and then, more and more young people will refuse to use existing provision. This 'retrenchment back to the office' syndrome is affecting practice. There is no doubt that it is leading some agencies to go up-market in their search for customers, accepting the 'middle-class homeless' for want of a better term to the detriment of those in greater need.

Some of the young people talked to emphasised this fact. They argued for a provision similar to a soup run aimed only at the young and stopping at those places where only the young predominate. This was seen as one practical way of supporting the young, getting in touch with many on the streets who were not being contacted, and allowing the young to be in contact with each other. It was argued that such a resource would help overcome some of the fear of authority that keeps some young people from contacting the agencies and would help workers relate directly to the needs of many young people who are not being helped at present.

Improving facilities for those in special need

Workers have outlined gaps in provision affecting different groups of young people. There is a need for more safe houses for some young people, somewhere that can offer them time and space to think over the issues. These are not seen as rivals to the provision set up by the CLTP, but rather a complementary service for older young people who do not want to contact home, and who may need that security to avoid becoming part of a more dangerous scenario.

There is some concern over the needs of young people who need time and space to explore issues around their own sexuality in an atmosphere that is non-threatening. They are seen to be at risk from others on the homeless circuit because of their sexual orientation and many workers fear that they are not using existing provision, despite clear efforts to make them welcome by the staff in the projects. A real safe house could provide these young people with a 'sanctuary' where they could be supported and helped.

Some accommodation is also necessary for those on drugs. Some would be highly supportive and give practical and emotional help to those waiting to go on a de-tox programme. Other provision could be based in small units that are not only for ex-drug users, so that those who have gone successfully through a programme can be given support to cope in the community. Such provision would not reject the individual at the first sign of a relapse, but would offer continual support to maintain a drug-free life.

There is also a glaring need for specialist accommodation for young people wanting to come off a life of prostitution. Young women especially would need the security of a safe house that could be private and secure and keep the pimps at bay. Young men might need less security, but just as much support. It is recognised that both these groups offer difficulties in working with them because of the reality that coming off prostitution can be a very gradual process. There is a need to accept that young people might well be actively involved in the life at various levels for some time after they have sought help. There is a scarcity of resources that can offer safety, support and a prostitution-free environment at present.

It is clear from statistics that are available that young people in care are most vulnerable to future homelessness and exploitation. Much of the work that can be done for them is preventative in nature. There is a need to review existing practice and policy for those leaving care. This has implications for the type of care offered to these young people and for the training of those working with them. First Key and other organisations in this area have been laying emphasis on this for a number of years. Care does not end at a chronological age. Some authorities have recognised this and are now offering opportunities for support for many years after, support that allows young people to opt in when necessary. Until it is accepted that such young people are an obligation to be met, they will continue to be a substantial percentage of London's homeless.

One aspect of accommodation that is absent at present is specialist provision for those young people who are suffering from the Aids virus. There is some anxiety about providing such a place, but there is no doubt that some of the young homeless may well be affected at present and will certainly die of the disease eventually. A hospice that cares for them and which allows them to live and die with dignity may soon be very necessary.

Finally, there are two groups of young people who are in need of a more intensive form of supervised accommodation than at present exists. The first are those who have grown up on dreadful housing estates, some of whom are children of single parents and some who may also belong to one of the ethnic minority groups. They are potentially very troublesome because of their anti-social attitudes, their depression and the difficulties they have experienced in school. Some may well have been through a variety of provision and dropped out. They need particular help with their anger, depression and hostility. They are often quite uncontrollable and violent, but they still need adults who can stick with them and be available for them.

The second group are young people who are at great risk of entering a life of crime, but who have not yet become part of the system. The Home Office is now ready to look at funding provision again for such groups after a moratorium of a number of years. Many of these young people commit petty crime in order to get support for their homelessness, but they do not necessarily need to be dealt with by the courts or the criminal justice system. With the need to keep people out of jails to reduce the prison population, it is felt by workers that such work would be given support. However, it is stressed that such work has to be combined with outreach facilities that could go straight to young people themselves and not necessarily rely on statutory referrals.

Organising the young
Susanna Agnelli (1986) advocated that street children become helpers and resources for their peers. It is widely accepted that,

if skilfully and carefully helped, young people can become an immense fund of support and practical help for each other. Agnelli argues that this type of support can help the individual 'reverse the terms of his relationship with his world' and 'liberate him from the tyranny of the peer group'.

The aim in all work with the young homeless is to help them take control of their situations instead of always being on the receiving end where other people and oppressive situations control their destiny. Agnelli argues that this is perhaps the only way of rehabilitating those young people who have already been alienated from society. In addition she feels that one way of setting these young people free is to ask something of them. 'The human heart is touched,' she says, 'not by being given something, but by having something asked of it.' This philosophy she argues is complementary to traditional ways of offering service, but it is largely unappreciated.

There is no doubt that this philosophy is very relevant to London's agencies. One of the consistent criticisms has been the failure to listen to the young and respond accordingly. That is why so many young people, it is felt, ignore what is on offer. There is a need not only to listen to the young, but to involve them actively in the organisation of the work to alleviate their plight and to help their fellows.

In this context, Brandon and his team (1980) argued, and they would receive a lot of support for this view still, that the 'here and now' may well be a vital mechanism for the young in coping with their deprivation and hardship, a necessary way of excluding, at least for the present, a potentially bleak future, by concentrating on the immediate. This runs counter to the philosophy of deferred gratification and planning which is the core of so much of the intervention practised by the agencies since the seventies. There is a need to understand that, at the point of contact, many young people need a support that is immediate and practical. Agencies have to understand this if they are to gear their services effectively and efficiently.

Improving the skills of the workers
There is no doubt that more than ever the young must feel that there is someone who is listening and willing to take action on their behalf. It has been stressed throughout this book that those who work with the young homeless in London show an immense

dedication to the task. A great deal of what exists does so because of the goodwill that is shown by paid staff and volunteers alike. It is this that overcomes the handicaps of poor facilities and under-funding.

However, more is needed if those who are presently not being helped by existing provision are to be reached. It is not an easy job. It demands skill, understanding and, most of all, patience to take on these young people on their own ground and win their trust. Agnelli (1986) argues that workers must have the inner strength to 'translate compassion into action'. She says that the most successful people in this work have always been those 'of exceptional vision and vigour, able to break through surly distrust and inspire deep loyalty'.

Establishing relationships with difficult, suspicious individuals and helping them to build bridges with society is not a nine-to-five job. For economic reasons much of the work in London can fall into this category. Too much emphasis can also be placed on the role of the volunteer, with little or no supportive training on an on-going basis for them. While there is an argument for the volunteer role, it cannot replace the skilled worker. Much more emphasis needs to be placed on this aspect of the work and efforts must be made to give supervision and training if workers are to recognise the values of the young homeless and see the world through their eyes.

There is no doubt that some people are anxious that this aspect of the task has been ignored in recent years. Brandon (1980) high-lighted it in the seventies and there is some validity still in the notion that there is too much political posturing that effectively gives the young homeless no voice. There is a danger that organ-isations can exist for their own benefit because they have ceased to listen to the young people they were set up to serve. As a result, the supports offered have been shunned by some young people who feel alone and abandoned. As one nineteen-year-old put it to a worker who saw him every evening on the way home from work, 'I'm no use to anyone. I cannot be helped by anyone. No one wants the likes of me'.

15 Conclusion

' "A little person is someone who starts something and a big person is someone who comes along and stops it." We must alter this image: a little person is someone who starts something and a big person is someone who helps to make it go.' (E J Anthony, *In Search of the Little People,* in *Children in Turmoil: Tomorrow's Parents.)*

No one can really say that they know the young homeless, no one, except themselves, can adequately speak for them and present their needs. What has been described in this book are impressions of lives, coloured as they are, by their often poignant and painful histories and the work that is carried out with and for them. The great diversity of work with and for young people often seems to split our attentions and energies into uncounted fragments, none of which seem to be related. The more needy the young person, the greater seems to be that diversity.

The task of working for and with young people is to make sense of that divergence and to bring an order and unity into their lives. The young cannot grow and achieve their potential in isolation. They need adults to guide them and to share their aspirations. Many of these young people have never had that guidance, that interest in them as individuals of worth. They have, consequently, lost trust in adults and have little belief in the society that has been bequeathed to them. There is a gulf that needs to be bridged with young people, and if that division is to become construction, there must be first of all an acknowledgement that they are not creatures from another planet, but our children, part of our world.

These young people do not belong to someone else. They are our concerns, our responsibility, and their plight is a reflection of how we order our society. We have to find ways of putting that across, not with research that passes over people's heads, but which touches the human element in all of us and brings home the concerns of these young people as being those of the whole society and of each of its members in particular as caring individuals.

There is a genuine fear among those who work with the young homeless that homelessness is fast becoming a 'trendy' problem, which all well meaning people should be seen to be concerned with. The worry is that such concern may do little towards an

understanding of the serious issues involved and will serve only
to ease the collective conscience. In the meantime the danger
increases of creating a society of young people who do not have
the opportunity to live in accommodation that is secure and which
they can call home.

Accommodation is not enough by itself. As our society becomes
increasingly materialistic, many of our young people are left with
little sense of purpose and nothing to look forward to. Many
workers argue that work for the homeless should be about
restoring this sense of purpose. A people approach rather than
a buildings approach is the way forward. The young must be given
back their futures and the wherewithal to live those futures in
a happy and fulfilled way. There is a plea for the professionals
to become involved and not sit on the sidelines offering platitudes
and expressions of concern. The young want good relationships
with caring adults who will believe in them and bring out their
potential.

In one of the interviews one lad put down this challenge.

'Try to survive from Friday evening to Monday morning, with
nowhere to live, no idea where your next meal is coming from,
with twenty pence in your pocket, and walk among those who
have money, who can sit down in restaurants or stand at the
bar of a pub. Look at their happiness and see how long it is
before you begin to be jealous and then hate them for it.'

This is the reality of so many of those who are young and
homeless in London, the nation's capital. If this was our youngster,
how would we feel, how would we respond?

This can be dismissed as a crude appeal to the emotions, yet
to offer supports that are constructive for these young people, we
have to respond with both heart and head. Somehow we can
never induce their growth or their healing; it will come only when
we move out in vision and action for them. That Dr Barnardo's,
and all those who have as their objective the welfare of the young,
might have this vision for the young homeless in London is the
purpose of this book and the plea from all those who have
contributed to it, so that

'. . . the Children who will find your doorway
Can stay a while,
And walk away knowing they, too, can dream.'

(The Heart of the Matter)

Appendices

Bibliography

AGNELLI, SUSANNA, *Street Children. A Growing Urban Tragedy,* Weidenfeld and Nicolson, London, 1986.

ALDRIDGE, DAVID, 'Children in Distress', *Crucible,* April/June 1985, pp 67-76.

ANDREWS, GEOFF, 'Scarman says Britain in Danger of Becoming a Slum Society', *The Guardian,* 6 January 1987.

ANDREWS, JANE, *Persistent Petty Offenders,* HMSO, London, 1981.

ANSELL, NEIL and POPPLEWELL, DAVID, *Two Years of Shelter: A Study of the Simon Community's Night Shelter,* The Simon Community, London, 1984.

ARCHARD, PETER, *Vagrancy, Alcoholism and Social Control,* Macmillan, London, 1979.

AULD, JOHN; DORN, NICHOLAS; and SOUTH, NIGEL, 'Heroin, Now Bringing it all Back Home', *Youth and Policy,* **9**, 1984, pp 1-7.

AUSTERBERRY, HELEN and WATSON, SOPHIE, *Women on the Margin. A Study of Single Women's Housing Problems,* The City University, London, 1984.

BALDWINSON, TONY, 'Turning a Blind Eye', *Youth in Society,* **105**, pp 16-18.

BARRY, NICOLA, 'Alcohol: The Major Public Health Issue of our Time', *Social Work Today,* 12 January 1987, pp 10-11.

BEACOCK, NICHOLAS, 'Campaigning for the Homeless and Rootless' in Cook, T. (ed), *Vagrancy. Some New Perspectives,* Academic Press, London, 1979, pp 119-40.

BERRIDGE, DAVID, *Children's Homes,* Blackwell, Oxford, 1985.

BERRY, DAVID, 'The Youth Problem', *New Society,* 24 April 1987, pp 16-17.

BEVINS, ANTHONY; BROWN, COLIN; KIRBY, TERRY; McKITHRICK, DAVID; PEARSON, ROSIE; and TIMMINS, NICHOLAS, 'Housing: The Hard Search for Solutions', *The Independent,* 21 October 1986.

BORGMAN, ROBERT, ' "Don't Come Home Again": Parental Banishment of Delinquent Youths', *Child Welfare,* **65**(3), 1986, pp 295-304.

BRANDON, D; WELLS, K; FRANCIS, C and RAMSEY, E, *The Survivors. A Study of Homeless Young Newcomers to London and the Responses Made to Them*, Routledge and Kegan Paul, London, 1980.

BRANGWYN, GILLIAN, 'Centre of Energy', *Social Work Today*, 19 March 1984, pp 10–11.

BRAUND, PHILIP and APPLEYARD, CHRISTINA, 'Children of Vice', *Daily Mirror*, 1 May 1987.

BROOKS, RICHARD and HANNA, MARK, 'Runaway Schoolgirls who Play a Dangerous Game', *The Observer*, 12 April 1987.

BROWN, GRAEME and MURCER, BILL, 'A Safe House amid Turmoil and Danger', *Community Care*, **649**, 1987, pp iv–v.

CARA, 'Irish Homeless and Rootless Project. Profile'. Unpublished Report.

CARA, 'Irish Homeless and Rootless Project. The Housing Position of Young Irish People in London'. Unpublished Report.

CHAPPELL, HELEN, 'The Rent Boy Scene', *New Society*, 31 October 1986, pp 8–9.

CHAR, *Replacing Night Shelters, CHAR Occasional Paper—5*, CHAR, London, 1985.

CLARK, MARK and DARLING, ALAN, *Leaving Home. A Training Manual for Workers with Young People*, The Scots Group, The IT Resource Centre, in conjunction with WECVS, Glasgow, 1986.

CLASSAF, *Board and Lodgings Regulations Conference. Workshop Notes*, 25 October 1985. GLC.

COOKE, LESLEY, 'Counselling House to Open', *Voluntary Voice*, **14**, 1987, p 6.

COSGROVE, ALEX (ed), *Housing and Young People. The Way Forward*, Blackrose Press, London, 1987.

COX, ALAISTAIR and COX, GABRIELLE, *Borderlines: A Partial View of Detached Work with Homeless Young People*, National Youth Bureau, London, 1977.

CRAN, JOHN, 'A Refuge for Young People', *Scottish Child*, **7**, 1985, pp 2–3.

DE SMIDT, GRAHAM and JANSEN, MINY, 'Homeless and Young People', *Youth and Policy*, **1**, 1983, pp 1–5.

DE'ATH, ERICA, 'The World of Runaways', *Community Care*, **649**, 1987, pp i–iii.

DE'ATH, ERICA and NEWMAN, CATHY, 'Children Who Run', *Children and Society*, **1**, 1987, pp 13–18.

DE'ATH, ERICA and SPARKS, IAN, 'See How They Run. Responses to Young Runaways', *Third Way*, **9**(12), 1986, pp 14–16.

DALRYMPLE, JAMES and BARWICK, SANDRA, 'The Gap Between Rich and Poor Grows Even Wider', *The Independent,* 29 January 1987.

DEER, BRIAN, 'Switch to Caravans may Ease the Homeless Crisis', *Sunday Times,* 22 March 1987.

DHSS; DES; HOME OFFICE; and MSC, *Misuse of Drugs with Special Reference to the Treatment and Rehabilitation of Misusers of Hard Drugs,* Government Response to the 4th Report from the Social Services Committee, Session 1984–85, HMSO, London, 1985.

DHSS, *Drug Misuse: Prevalence and Service Provision,* HMSO, London, 1985.

DHSS, *Working Group on Homeless Young People Report,* HMSO, London, 1976.

DHSS, *Heroin Misuse. Campaign Evaluation,* Research Bureau Ltd, London, 1986.

DORN, NICHOLAS and SOUTH, NIGEL, *Helping Drug Users,* Gower, Aldershot, 1985.

DRAKE, MADELINE; O'BRIEN, MAUREEN; and BIEBREYCK, TONY, *Single and Homeless,* HMSO, London, 1982.

DUGGAN, MARIA, *Report of Research regarding the Establishment of a Specialist Unit to Co-ordinate Services to Prostitute Women,* 30 May 1984. London Borough of Camden.

DUN, ELIZABETH, 'Seeking a Cure', *Community Care,* 12 March 1987, p 23.

EATON, LYNN and PERKS, BEN, 'Telling it Like it is', *Social Work Today,* 6 October 1986, pp 12–13.

ELLIOT, VALERIE, ' "Blacklist" of Homes Left Empty Urged', *London Daily News,* 31 March 1987.

FISCHER, PAMELA J and BREAKEY, WILLIAM R, 'Homelessness and Mental Health: An Overview', *International Journal of Mental Health,* **14**(4), pp 6–41.

FRANKS, ALAN, 'Down and Out of Sight . . . ', *The Times,* 14 January 1987.

FRIEND, MELANIE, *Single and Homeless in Hackney,* Trojan Press, London, 1984.

GAY, MARTYN, 'Drug and Solvent Abuse in Adolescents', *Nursing Times,* 26 January 1986, pp 34–35.

GLANCEY, JONATHAN, 'Homes. Brent Sets the Pace', *London Daily News,* 23 April 1987.

GREATER LONDON TRADE UNION RESOURCE UNIT, *Homes and Jobs,* London, 1986.

GREVE, JOHN, *Investigation into Homelessness in London. Interim Report*, University of Leeds, Leeds, 1985.

GREVE, JOHN, *Homelessness in London. Working Paper 60*, Bristol School for Advanced Urban Studies, Bristol, 1986.

GROSSKURTH, ANN, 'From Care to Nowhere', *Roof*, July/August 1984, pp 11–14.

HARRIS, MARTYN, 'When one Young Man Lived in a Shoe', *Daily Telegraph*, 27 January 1987.

HARTNOLL, RICHARD, 'Recent Trends in Drug Use in Britain', *Druglink*, July/August 1986, pp 12–13.

HENCKE, DAVID, 'Homelessness Doubles to 100,000 Figure', *The Guardian*, 10 April 1987.

HENCKE, DAVID, 'Patten Admits High Cost of B & B for Homeless', *The Guardian*, 17 January 1987.

HILDITCH, STEVE, *Ordinary People. Homeless in the Housing Crisis*, Shelter, London, 1982.

HOLMES, GODFREY, 'Board out of Their Minds', *Community Care*, **568**, 1985, p 13.

HOLROYD, DAVID, 'Drug Abuse and the Role of the Local Authorities', *Municipal Journal*, 25 April 1986, pp 664–5.

HOME OFFICE, *Police and Criminal Evidence Act 1984: Codes of Practice*, HMSO, London, 1985.

HOWARTH, VALERIE, *A Survey of Families in Bed and Breakfast Hotels*, Report to the Governors of the Thomas Coram Foundation, April 1987.

HOWIE, DAVID and BALDWINSON, TONY, 'Leaving Home—A Youth Work Response', *Youth in Society*, **109**, 1985, pp 20–21.

INSTITUTE FOR THE STUDY OF DRUG DEPENDENCE, 'Heroin in Britain', *Druglink*, May/June 1986, pp 9–12.

IVES, RICHARD, 'What is Behind the Figures on Solvent Abuse?', *Community Care*, **645**, pp 10–11.

JACOBS, ANNE and WATERHOUSE, ROSIE, 'Costly Scandal of the Bed and Breakfast Trap', *Sunday Times*, 11 January 1987.

JAMIESON, ANNE; GLANZ, ALAN; and MACGREGOR, SUSANNE, *Dealing with Drug Misuse. Crisis Intervention in the City*, Tavistock, London, 1984.

JANSEN, MINY and DE SMIDT, GRAHAM, 'Young and Homeless', *Roof*, May/June 1982, pp 17–20.

JOHNSON, HEATHER, 'Bad Law, Bad Housing', *Voluntary Voice*, **14**, 1987, pp 8–9.

JONES, DAVID R, *Nowhere Else to Go. Young People and Street Offences*, Report using Research by Jeff Evans, Soho Project and WECVS, London, 1986.

JONES, GEORGE, 'Homeless Offered Shelter', *Daily Telegraph*, 15 January 1987.

KENNEDY, STANISLAUS (ed), *Streetwise. Homelessness Among the Young in Ireland and Abroad*, The Glendale Press, Dublin, 1987.

KILEEN, DAMIAN, 'The Young Runaways', *New Society*, 17 January 1986, pp 97–98.

LAWRENCE, JEREMY, 'Society Services. The Fall Out from Care', *New Society*, 8 March 1984, p 379.

LEE, MARK; RUDD, LESLIE; and BARRETT, JANIS, *Going West. Working with Young Problem Drug Users on the Streets of Central London*, An Account of the Detached Youth Worker Post at the Hungerford Drug Project, Turning Point, London, 1987.

LEONARD, JOHN, 'Hotels of Heartbreak', *London Daily News*, 30 March 1987, p 5.

LIPSEY, DAVID, 'Marriage Break ups Fuel Homes Crisis', *New Society*, 30 January 1987, p 7.

LIVINGSTONE, KEN, *GLC Housing Research and Policy Report—1, Homelessness in London: A Report by the Leader of the GLC*, GLC, London, 1985.

LOCKS, CELIA, '50p Beggars who Ponce for a Living', *The Guardian*, 5 May 1987.

LUPTON, CAROL, *Moving Out. Older Teenagers Leaving Residential Care*, Social Services Research and Intelligence Unit, Portsmouth, 1985.

MANNING, P and REDLINGER, L, 'Drugs as Work', *Research in the Sociology of Work: Peripheral Workers (2)*, JAI Press, Greenwich, Conn, 1983.

MARR, ANDREW, 'Ridley Blamed for Chaos in Housing the Homeless', *The Independent*, 13 March 1987.

MASON-JOHN, VALERIE, 'Voting with Their Feet', *Community Care*, **644**, p 10.

MCCORMACK, ARLENE; JANUS, MARK-DAVID; and BURGESS, ANN WOLBERT, 'Runaway Youths and Sexual Victimization: Gender Differences in an Adolescent Runaway Population', *Child Abuse and Neglect*, **10**(3), 1986, pp 387–95.

MCKECHNIE, SHEILA, 'Raising the Roof on the Right to a Home', *London Daily News*, 3 April 1987.

McMULLAN, RITCHIE J, 'Youth Prostitution: A Balance of Power?', *Journal of Adolescence*, **10**(1), 1987, pp 35-43.

McMULLAN, RITCHIE J, 'The Cycle of Sexual Abuse and Rape of Boys Involved in Prostitution', *Youth and Policy*, **23**, 1988, pp 35-42.

MEACHER, MICHAEL, *Cold Comfort. Alcohol/Drugs/Homelessness*, House of Commons, London, 1984.

NACRO, *Homeless Young Offenders. An Action Programme*, NACRO, London, 1981.

NASH, IAN, 'Teaching Life's Casualties the Art of Survival', *Times Educational Supplement*, 5 December 1986, p 10.

NATIONAL CHILDREN'S HOMES, *Children in Danger: A NCH Factfile about Children Today*, NCH, London, 1982.

NEWMAN, CATHY, 'Statistics of Survival', *Community Care*, **649**, 1987, pp vi-vii.

NEWCOMBE, RUSSELL, 'High Time for Harm Reduction', *Druglink*, January/February 1987, pp vi-vii.

ORR, DAVID, 'Views of Homelessness', *Centrepoint Annual Report 1984*, London, p 5.

PARISH, AMANDA, *Resourcing Young People's Housing*, The Report of a Consultation about a Resource Centre concerned with the Housing Needs of Young People, The Young Homelessness Group, March 1987.

PIENAAR, JOHN, 'Ridley may Force Aid for Homeless', *The Independent*, 5 March 1987.

PRITCHARD, COLIN; FIELDING, MARY; CHOUDRY, N; COX, MALCOLM; and DIAMOND, IAN, 'Incidence of Drug and Solvent Abuse in "Normal" Fourth and Fifth Year Comprehensive School Children—some Socio-behavioural Characteristics', *British Journal of Social Work*, **16**, 1986, pp 341-51.

PRYKE, PETER, 'Young Homeless should Quit London says Ridley', *Daily Telegraph*, 5 March 1987.

PURKIS, ANDREW and HODSON, PAUL, *Housing and Community Care*, National Council for Voluntary Organisations Policy Analysis Unit, London, 1982.

PYRAMID PROJECT, *Homelessness and Camden's Young People . . . What Can We Do?'*, Unpublished Report on a Day Conference, 10 April 1987.

RICE, ROBERT, 'Tube Shelters as Homes Plan', *The Independent*, 24 January 1987.

ROBERTS, ANN; SHEPPARD, ERIC and WILSON, VERONICA (eds), *Participation in Prevention. The International Youth Forum on Alcohol and Drugs, Cyncoed Conference Centre, Cardiff, 9–12 July 1985.* Council for Wales of Voluntary Youth Services, Cardiff, 1986.

ROBERTSON, SHELAGH and MATHESON, CAM, *Enforcing Vagrancy,* WECVS Special Report, London, 1986.

SAUNDERS, BARBARA, *Homeless Young People in Britain. The Contribution of the Voluntary Sector,* NCVO Bedford Square Press, London, 1986.

SCOTT, JACKIE, 'Streets of Shame', *Youth Service Scene,* September 1985, pp 5–8.

SCOTTISH HEALTH EDUCATION GROUP, *Drugs and Young People in Scotland,* 3rd ed, Scottish Health Education Group, Edinburgh, 1986.

SEABROOK, JENNY, 'Homing Instinct at Home around the World', *The Guardian,* 23 March 1987.

SERENY, GITTA, *The Invisible Children: Child Prostitution in America, Germany and Britain,* Andre Deutsch, London, 1984.

SHARRON, HOWARD, 'Out of House and Home', *Social Work Today,* 25 March 1985, pp 12–16.

SHERMAN, JILL, 'Call for Action on Young Homeless', *The Times,* 7 January 1987.

SHOTTON, TIM, 'Rights of Homeless Young People', *Childright,* **18**, 1985, pp 9–11.

SMITH, DAVID, 'No Place Like Home', *Youth in Society,* **104**, 1985, pp 11–14.

SMITH, DOUGLAS, *The Police and Criminal Evidence Act 1984: A Brief Guide for Youth Workers,* The National Youth Bureau, London, 1986.

SNELLGROVE, BRIAN (ed), *Report of a Meeting of Experts in Various Fields Invited to Give Their Views on the Current Homelessness Situation—18th February 1987,* Sutton, 1987.

SOCIAL SERVICES CORRESPONDENT, 'Growing Plight of London's Destitutes', *The Independent,* 20 March 1987.

SPICER, FAITH, 'Reflections on the Past: The London Youth Advisory Centre', *Counselling,* **54**, 1985, pp 6–8.

STEELE, DON, 'Alcohol and Drugs—Unsuitable Attachment?', *Druglink,* September/October 1986, p 7.

STEIN, MIKE, 'Young, single and homeless', *Social Services Insight,* 19 June 1987, pp 18–20.

176 A CAPITAL OFFENCE

STERN, JONATHAN and PAWSON, HAL, 'London Hotel Homeless', *Voluntary Voice*, **17**, 1987, p 1.

STRANG, DR JOHN, 'Changing the Image of the Drug Taker', *Health and Social Services Journal*, **94**, 1984, pp 1202–1204.

SUTHERLAND, IAN, 'The Place is the Place', *Community Care*, **557**, pp 21–23.

SUTTON, ELAINE and CARRIER, JANE, *No Room to Move*, Threshold Housing Advice Centre, London, 1987.

SWEENEY, JOHN, 'Down and Out in St James's, *New Society*, 30 January 1987, pp 8–9.

THE CENTRAL LONDON OUTREACH TEAM, *Sleeping Out in Central London*, GLC, London, 1984.

THE HOUSING CORPORATION, *Regional Strategy Statement 1987–1992: London and the Home Counties North*, The Housing Corporation, 1986.

TIRBUTT, SUSAN, 'Hotel Group is Charging Double Rate for Accommodating the Homeless, *The Guardian*, 23 January 1987.

WATERS, JACQUELINE, *The Nature of Single Homelessness*, University of East Anglia, Norwich, 1982.

WOLMAR, CHRISTIAN, 'Homeless Forced on to Streets to Make Way for Hotel Tourists, *London Daily News*, 22 April 1987.

Moving Out, Smith Bundy Video, London, 1986.

YAPP, ANGELA, *First Come, First Served. A Study of Emergency Night Shelters*, Resource Information Services, London, 1987.

Reports

Bed and Breakfast Project and Survey of Non-Priority Homeless in Camden, Report by the Director of Housing, Private Sector Sub-Committee, 17 June 1987. London Borough of Camden.

'Child Prostitution a Target', *Social Work Today*, 4 May 1987, p 3.

Female Prostitution. A Report by the Street Level Team, The Church Army, London, 1986.

History is Ours. Writings from a Youth Centre in the West End of London, New Horizon Youth Centre, London, 1985.

Homelessness Statistics 1985–86 Actuals, The Chartered Institute of Public Finance and Accountability, London, 1986.

'Homeless Total may be 250,000', *The Independent*, 11 April 1987.

Housing: A Fair Deal for Youth, Report of the Seminar on Housing Organised by the International Youth Year (England), December 1986.

Housing and Homelessness: Report of the Social Policy Committee of the Board for Social Responsibility, CIO Publishing, London, 1982.

'Housing: The Hard Search for Solutions', *The Independent*, 21 October 1986.

Local Housing Statistics. England and Wales. January 1980–January 1987, HMSO, London, 1987.

Misuse of Drugs with Special Reference to the Treatment and Rehabilitation of Misusers of Hard Drugs: 4th Report from the Social Services Committee, Session 1984–85: Together with the Proceedings of the Committee and Minutes of Evidence. HMSO, London, 1985.

Moving on Moving in. Working Towards Proper Housing for Young People, A Report by the Young Homelessness Group, January 1985.

People Sleeping Rough in Central London, Report by Head of Housing Services, GLC Single Homeless Sub-Committee, 17 November 1983.

Single Problem. Homelessness and Single People, Single Problem Housing Campaign, November 1984.

The Cold Weather Crisis, January 1987, A Report on the Activities and Recommendations for the Future. WECVS, London, 1987.

'Under Pressure', *Childright*, **33**, 1987, pp 16–17.

Annual Reports

A Better Housing Deal for Black People. Federation of Black Housing Associations, 1986.

Alone in London Service. Bi-Annual Report, 1983–85.

Alone in London Service, 1985–86.

Centrepoint Soho, 1985 and 1986.

City Roads, Crisis Intervention. A Team Approach, 1984–85 and 1985–86.

Getting Somewhere, Piccadilly Advice Centre and the Leaving Home Project, ISCL Report 1985.

ISCL Annual Report 1985–86, Piccadilly Advice Centre and the Leaving Home Project.

New Horizon Youth Centre Ltd, 1985–86.

Off Centre, 1984–85 and 1985–86.

Short Stay Youth Homeless Project, April 1985–March 1986.

Thamesreach, 1985–86.

The London Irish Centre. Annual Welfare Reports, 1984 and 1986.

Ujima Housing Association, 1985–86.

WECVS, 1986.

Young Homeless Group, 1986.

Contacts

Visits
1 Caroline Abrahams and Roddy Mungall, Researchers, National Children's Homes, Streatham.
2 Emlyn Jones, Director, and Tony May, National Association of Voluntary Hostels, Covent Garden.
3 Bill Murcer, Principal Officer, The Children's Society, Peckham.
4 Paul Kobrak, The Young Homelessness Group, London WC1.
5 Sergeant Tony Heath, Juvenile Protection Bureau, Vine Street, Soho.
6 Mark Fittock, Manager, Dean Street Hostel, Soho.
7 Sue Lipscombe, Westminster Social Services, Bruce House, London WC2.
8 Mick Baker, Leader, Soho Project, London WC2.
9 Julia Unwin, Co-ordinator, West End Co-ordinated Voluntary Service for Homeless Single People. London WC2.
10 Bryan Symons, Director, Alone in London Service, Euston.
11 Peter Molyneaux, External Liaison Worker, Piccadilly Advice Centre, Shaftesbury Avenue.
12 Norman Gay, Social Worker, 'Off Centre' Project, Hackney.
13 Martin Jones and Rupert Chandler, Leaving Home Project, Shaftesbury Avenue.
14 Nick Hardwick, Director, Centrepoint, London WC2.
15 Ken Coleman, Assistant Director, Westminster Social Services.
16 Killian Lumpe, Day Team Leader, Area 5, Westminster Social Services.
17 Berry Rance, Project Worker, New Horizon Day Centre, London WC2.
18 Margaret Weston, Manager, Birkenhead Street Hostel, Kings Cross.
19 Julia Percival, Director, and Eileen Hawkins, Chairperson, The London Council for the Welfare of Women and Girls, Bloomsbury.
20 Seamus Taylor, Project Worker, The Irish Centre, Camden.
21 Kuma Mehta, Out of Hours Team Leader, Area 5, Westminster Social Services.
22 Ritchie McMullan, Director, Streetwise Project, Earls Court.
23 John Broadbent, HM Youth Inspectorate, Soho.

24 Richard Wiseman, Co-ordinator, Short Stay Young Homeless Project, Holloway Road.
25 Sheila O'Connor, Dave Gilmour, Probation Officers, Rathbone Place, London W1.
26 Mark Lee, Outreach Worker, Hungerford Drug Project, Charing Cross.
27 Alaistair Pettygrew, Assistant Director, Children's Services, and Stephen Barber, Principal Officer, Specialist Services with Community Services, Kensington and Chelsea Social Services.
28 John Lane, Director, St Mungo's Association, London WC2.
29 Alison Mernagh, James Dougan and Ruth Shelton, the Independent Living Project, Hammersmith and Fulham Social Services.
30 Father Bill Kirkpatrick, Manager, Streetwise Project, Earls Court.
31 Alan Davidson, Project Leader, The Alone in London Counselling Service, London WC1.
32 Nick Fenton, Deputy Director, The Mental Health Foundation, London W1.
33 Mrs Pearce, Director, the House of St Barnabas, Soho.
34 Bill Moore, Co-ordinator, HASSLL (Homeless Against Social Security Lodging Laws), Camden.
35 Ossie Nobleman, Director, Mixifren Housing Association, Hackney.
36 Inspector Shaw, West End Juvenile Bureau.
37 Greg Ince, Co-ordinator of the Homeless Youth Project, Waltham Forest.
38 Dudley Burke, Project Worker, Short Stay Young Homeless Project, Earls Court.
39 Jane Coleman, Leader, Church Army Street Level Team, London WC1.
40 Jill Johnson, Project Leader, Bridges Project, National Children's Homes, Hatfield.
41 Tony Soares, Director and Sonia McIntosh, Co-ordinator, Ujima Housing Aid Centre, Kilburn.
42 Jeremy Swain, Outreach Worker, Thamesreach, Charing Cross.
43 Brian Rickets, Project Worker, Housing Services Agency, Kings Cross.
44 Mervyn Dawkins, Senior Probation Officer, Inner London Probation Service, Victoria.

45 Maria Duggan, Social Worker, Camden Social Services.
46 Louise Flynn, Project Worker, The Pyramid Project, Save The Children Fund, Kentish Town.
47 Leah Davidson, Practice Co-ordinator, City Roads Crisis Intervention Centre, Islington.
48 Brother Sam Symister, Director, Harambee 11 Project, Hackney.
49 Sister Barbara, Leader, Passage Day Centre, Victoria.
50 Hattie Llewellyn Davies, Special Needs Housing Group, Victoria and Chair of the Youth Homelessness Group.
51 Ken Livingstone, Labour MP for Brent East and former Leader of the GLC.
52 Mr Indran, Housing Manager and Simon Lukes, Housing Worker, The Hackney Short Life Users Group.
53 Superintendent King and Chief Inspector Saunders, Railway Police HQ, Tavistock Place.
54 Chief Inspector Atkinson, Railway Police, Euston Station.
55 Acting Chief Inspector Excell, Victoria Station Railway Police.
56 Graeme Brown, Project Leader, Central London Teenage Project.
57 Mary Boyle, Housing Manager, CARA, The Irish Homeless and Rootless Project, Holloway.
58 Sister Rachel, Salvation Army Midnight Patrol, Kings Cross.
59 Seema Sodhi, Volunteer Worker, Centrepoint, Shaftesbury Avenue.
60 Emma Marks, Project Worker, Centrepoint, Shaftesbury Avenue.
61 Sue Newman, Inspector, DHSS, Euston.
62 Vernon Clarke, Race Equality Officer, Federation of Black Housing Associations, Tottenham.

Phoned
63 Clare Croft-Whyte, Project Worker, Inner City Action on Drugs, London N1.
64 Alan George and Elaine Sutton, Threshold Centre, Uxbridge and Wandsworth.
65 Robina Rafferty, Catholic Housing Aid Society, Old Brompton Road, London SW5.
66 Gilbert Haywood, Social Work Co-ordinator, West London Mission, London W1.

67 Dana Blair, Project Worker, Alcohol Recovery Project, Kings Cross.
68 Paul Robson, First Key Association, London SE1.
69 Dr Pat Logan, Southwark Diocesan Council for Social Aid, Camberwell.
70 Riverpoint Single Homeless Project, Hammersmith.
71 Liz Pritchard, Manager, North Lambeth Day Centre, Waterloo.
72 Ian Ramsbottom, Project Worker, Providence Row Hostel, London E1.
73 Mr Vieira, Administrator, Barons Court Project Day Centre, London W14.
74 Ron Nott, Project Leader, St Anselms Community Project, Southall.
75 Kevin Wright, Project Leader, Intake, London WC1.
76 Isobel Robertson, Co-ordinated Accommodation Scheme, London SE1.
77 Advisory Service for Squatters, London N1.
78 Mrs Deacon, Project Leader, Countour, Lavender Hill, London SW11.
79 Denise Little, Rehousing/Resettlement Worker, West London Cyrenians, London W11.
80 Joan Ferguson, Housing Manager, Patchwork Community, London N1.
81 Dave Jones, Stopover, Lewisham.